GEORGIA TRIVIA

GEORGIA TRIVIA

COMPILED BY
ERNIE & JILL COUCH

Rutledge Hill Press
Nashville, Tennessee

Published by Rutledge Hill Press, Inc., 513 Third Avenue South, Nashville, Tennessee 37210

Typography by Bailey Typography, Inc. and ProtoType Graphics, Inc.
Cover photography by Doug Brachey Photography
Color separation by Manning Camera Graphics
Book and cover design by Ernie Couch / Consultx

Library of Congress Cataloging-in-Publication Data

Couch, Ernie, 1949-
    Georgia trivia.

    1. Georgia—Miscellanea.   2. Questions and answers.
I. Couch, Jill, 1948-   . II. Title.
F286.5.C68   1986   975.8   86-15423
ISBN 0-934935-21-7

Printed in the United States of America
3 4 5 6 7 8 - 90 89 88

PREFACE

As the paramount of both Classic and New South, Georgia stands as a blend of age old traditions, steeped in hospitality, and the latest in high-tech advancement. Georgia's colorful and compelling history speaks of a richly diversified land and people. Captured within these pages are some of the highlights of this rich heritage, both the known and the not so well known.

Georgia Trivia is designed to be informative, educational and entertaining. But most of all we hope that you will be motivated to learn more about the great state of Georgia.

Ernie & Jill Couch

To
Mary Bray Wheeler,
Berry Henderson Couch
and
the great people of Georgia

TABLE OF CONTENTS

GEOGRAPHY

C H A P T E R   O N E

Q. How many counties are there in Georgia?

A. 159 counties.

◆

Q. The annual Miss Georgia Pageant is hosted by what city?

A. Columbus.

◆

Q. Which county is the youngest in the state?

A. Peach County, created July 18, 1924.

◆

Q. In which time zone is Georgia situated?

A. Eastern.

◆

Q. Where is the tallest hotel building in the world found?

A. Atlanta, Peachtree Center Plaza, 723 feet, a total of 71 stories.

Q. Which community is the "Apple Capital of Georgia"?

A. Ellijay.

———◆———

Q. Which states border Georgia?

A. Florida, Alabama, Tennessee, North Carolina and South Carolina.

———◆———

Q. What does the town name Dahlonega mean in the Cherokee language?

A. "Precious yellow metal"—gold.

———◆———

Q. Where was the great novel *Gone with the Wind* written?

A. In Atlanta, on Crescent Avenue.

———◆———

Q. Where is the Peach Blossom Trail situated?

A. On US 341 north of Perry.

———◆———

Q. In the 1890s what was the communal type society established in Ware County called?

A. Ruskin.

———◆———

Q. Which museum, featuring over 30 historical airplanes, is situated in Warner Robins?

A. Robins Air Force Base Museum of Aviation.

Q. The South's largest Civil War period sword factory was situated in what city?

A. Columbus.

Q. What is the name of the lower region of Charlton County, which is bordered on three sides by the state of Florida?

A. Big Bend.

Q. What is President Jimmy Carter's hometown?

A. Plains.

Q. What neighborhood has the distinction of being Atlanta's first suburb?

A. Inman Park, circa 1890.

Q. The world's second bottler of Coca-Cola, E. R. Barber, was from what Georgia city?

A. Valdosta.

Q. What is the total land and inland water area of the state?

A. 58,910 square miles.

Q. What river forms much of the northeastern boundary of the state?

A. Savannah River.

Q. How long is the Georgia section of the Appalachian Trail?

A. 78 miles.

———◆———

Q. Albany was named for the capital city of what state?

A. New York.

———◆———

Q. What is the name of the farm complex southeast of Juliette that was run from the 1840s to the 1940s and is now open to the public?

A. Jarrell Plantation.

———◆———

Q. Where was Confederate hero William Thomas Overby born?

A. About ten miles east of Newnan.

———◆———

Q. Helen is recognized for what type of architecture?

A. Bavarian Alpine architecture.

———◆———

Q. What name was given in 1926 to the 280 acre juvenile detention house development situated in Bibb County?

A. Smithsonia.

———◆———

Q. Why has Georgia been called the "Empire State of the South"?

A. Because of its large size and thriving industries.

Q. The Blood Mountain Archeological Area in Union County was the site of a great battle between what two Indian tribes prior to the arrival of the white man?

A. Cherokee and Creek Indians.

Q. Under the Confederacy, what city served as the temporary state capital from November 18, 1864 to March 11, 1865?

A. Macon.

Q. What establishment is the largest employer in the state?

A. Robins Air Force Base.

Q. Where did Mercer Institute, which later became Mercer University, open in 1833?

A. Penfield.

Q. What is the greatest distance north to south in the state?

A. 315 miles.

Q. What river forms the border between the southeastern corner of Georgia and the northeastern corner of Florida?

A. St. Marys River.

Q. Which town is known as the "City of Thirteen Highways"?

A. Hawkinsville.

Q. What is the name of the South's largest department store, located in Atlanta?

A. Rich's Department Store.

———◆———

Q. Which county borders both Alabama and Florida?

A. Seminole County.

———◆———

Q. Where is the antebellum house of Alexander H. Stephens, Vice President of the Confederacy, located?

A. Crawfordville.

———◆———

Q. Approximately what percentage of Georgia's population is urban?

A. 60 per cent.

———◆———

Q. From which two counties was a total of 255 square miles taken to form Ben Hill County on July 31, 1906?

A. Irwin and Wilcox counties.

———◆———

Q. Covering 28,000 acres, what is the largest campus in the world?

A. Berry College.

———◆———

Q. What Monroe County community, established in 1966, is named for the type of cotton fabric produced by the Bibb Manufacturing Company for the manufacturing of sheets and pillow cases?

A. Percale.

Q. In 1861 the legislature of Georgia changed the name of which county to Bartow, to honor Confederate hero Colonel Francis S. Bartow?

A. Cass County.

———◆———

Q. What is the nickname of Athens?

A. "Classic City."

———◆———

Q. For whom is 2,990-foot-high Charlie Mountain in Rabun County named?

A. Charlie Hicks, a principal Cherokee chief.

———◆———

Q. Where is the National Center for Disease Control?

A. Atlanta.

———◆———

Q. Which county was formed in 1856 by taking acreage from Coffee, Irwin and Lowndes counties?

A. Berrien County.

———◆———

Q. Which state park, located in Bartow County, was developed in the 1930s for blacks?

A. George Washington Carver State Park.

———◆———

Q. An 1883 steam pumper for fire fighting, one of the oldest in the world, may be seen in what community?

A. Hawkinsville.

Q. Where can you see the Eagle Rock Effigy, a 10-foot-high mound of milky quartz shaped like an outstretched bird with a 120-foot wingspread, approximately 6,000 years old?

A. Eatonton.

———◆———

Q. What log structure situated on the north edge of Riverdale was designated Federal headquarters in August, 1864, from which generals Sherman and Thomas transmitted and received dispatches?

A. The Drew Couch house.

———◆———

Q. What community in Dougherty County was given its name because of being located in the center of the world's leading paper shell pecan region?

A. Pecan City.

———◆———

Q. Which ocean borders Georgia?

A. The Atlantic Ocean.

———◆———

Q. Which is Georgia's southernmost coastal island?

A. Cumberland Island.

———◆———

Q. What town, situated 1,395 feet above sea level, is named for the Italian word meaning "high"?

A. Alto.

———◆———

Q. Upon its completion in 1927, the Juliette Grist Mill held what world record?

A. World's largest water powered grist mill.

Q. Due to the moderate climate, by what nickname is the southeastern region of the United States, which includes Georgia, known?

A. The Sunbelt.

———◆———

Q. What town is situated at the junction of Bleckley, Laurens, Twiggs and Wilkinson counties?

A. Allentown.

———◆———

Q. The only Georgia representative to be crowned Miss America, Neva Jane Langley, was from what city?

A. Macon.

———◆———

Q. What community, situated in Wheeler County, is named for the famous San Antonio, Texas, mission meaning "cottonwood" or "poplar" in Spanish?

A. Alamo.

———◆———

Q. Where is the world's largest aircraft plant under one roof located?

A. Marietta, Lockheed Aircraft.

———◆———

Q. For what is Modoc in Emmanuel County named?

A. A northwestern Indian tribe.

———◆———

Q. In what county was noted author Erskine Caldwell born?

A. Coweta County.

Q. Which town states that it is the "Garden Spot of the World and Southwest Georgia"?

A. Arlington.

Q. Where was the last official business of the Confederate States Treasury transacted?

A. Sandersville.

Q. What city is the capital of Georgia?

A. Atlanta.

Q. What has been the location of the Georgia School for the Deaf since its first five students were admitted in 1846?

A. Cave Springs.

Q. The 132-foot-long Cromer's Mill covered bridge of town lattice design, built in 1906, is located in which county?

A. Franklin County.

Q. By what name was the coastal plain of Georgia known to the Spanish?

A. Gaule, pronounced "Wally."

Q. The Georgia state legislature consists of how many representatives?

A. 180 state representatives.

Q. What plantation was the largest and most famous of the St. Simons antebellum plantations?

A. The Hamilton Plantation.

———◆———

Q. By what name is the convergence of several major thoroughfares that form Atlanta's hub known?

A. Five Points.

———◆———

Q. Waycross is located in what county?

A. Ware County.

———◆———

Q. What Clay County town is known as the "Queen City of the Chattahoochee"?

A. Fort Gaines.

———◆———

Q. For whom was the town of Mitchell named?

A. R. M. Mitchell, president of the Augusta Southern Railroad.

———◆———

Q. What is the "Candy Capital of Georgia"?

A. Eastman.

———◆———

Q. Which original county was first organized as the Parish of St. George?

A. Burke County.

Q. Where was a branch of the United States mint operated for 23 years for the purpose of striking gold coins?

A. Dahlonega.

———————◆———————

Q. Where was the Georgia Baptist Convention organized on June 27, 1822?

A. Powelton.

———————◆———————

Q. For whom was Fort Frederica on St. Simons Island named?

A. Frederick Louis, Prince of Wales.

———————◆———————

Q. A Confederate gun shop originally was moved to which two Georgia towns during the Civil War?

A. Rome and Dawson.

———————◆———————

Q. Which town is known as "The Broiler City"?

A. Canton.

———————◆———————

Q. What college is situated at Statesboro?

A. Georgia Southern.

———————◆———————

Q. Black Rock Mountain State Park is situated in what town in Rabun County?

A. Mountain City.

Q. What is the nickname of Albany?

A. "City of Opportunity."

Q. The misreading of a post office application in Washington, D.C., for the Georgia Community of Fox Valley in 1825 brought about what automatic name change?

A. A change to the name Fort Valley.

Q. Where is the Cyclorama located?

A. Grant Park, Atlanta.

Q. What was the name of the post office established June 9, 1835 on the site of present-day Atlanta?

A. White Hall.

Q. What body of water borders Clay, Quitman and Stewart counties on the west?

A. The Walter F. George Reservoir or Lake George.

Q. The whimsically named community of Hopeulikit is situated in what county?

A. Bulloch County.

Q. What is the location of Georgia Southwestern College?

A. Americus.

Q. The Army's Fort Stewart is situated in which county?

A. Liberty.

———◆———

Q. What are the state colors?

A. Red, white and blue.

———◆———

Q. Captain William A. Fuller, the Western and Atlantic Railroad conductor who led the recapturing of the *General*, stolen by Andrew's Raiders at Big Shanty, April 12, 1862, was born in what city?

A. Morrow.

———◆———

Q. What waterway threads its way through the state's coastal islands?

A. The Atlantic Intracoastal Waterway.

———◆———

Q. Arnold Blum, who helped the United States win the 1957 Walker Cup Crown, is a native of what community?

A. Macon.

———◆———

Q. What community in Carroll County carries the name of a state?

A. Kansas.

———◆———

Q. What is the name of the four-year Bible College at Toccoa, designed for students from missionary families living all over the world?

A. Toccoa Falls Institute.

Q. Where is the oldest continually used courthouse in the state?

A. Fayette County Courthouse, built in 1825 in Fayetteville.

———◆———

Q. For whom was Clarksville named?

A. Governor John C. Clark, 1819—1823.

———◆———

Q. Approximately how long is the Georgia coastline?

A. 100 miles.

———◆———

Q. Where was the home of General Jordan Bush, who as the last Confederate veteran from Georgia died in 1952 at the age of 107?

A. Fitzgerald.

———◆———

Q. What community about ten miles north of Valdosta is named for the Indian word meaning "much water"?

A. Mineola.

———◆———

Q. What was the most expensive British fortification built in North America?

A. Fort Frederica, St. Simons Island.

———◆———

Q. Known as "the Christmas Town of Georgia," which town features streets with Christmas-related names?

A. Bethlehem.

Q. Cairo is noted for being the center of what type of trade in the state?

A. The syrup trade.

◆

Q. What was the name of the first Scottish colony in Georgia, situated in McIntosh County?

A. New Inverness, later renamed Darien.

◆

Q. Near which present-day town was the "Great Buffalo Lick" located?

A. Philomath.

◆

Q. The majority of the Okefenokee Swamp is situated in which two counties?

A. Charlton and Ware Counties.

◆

Q. Where was the largest and most effective private armory in the Confederacy located?

A. Athens, Cook and Brother Armory.

◆

Q. Moultrie is located on what river?

A. The Ocklockney River.

◆

Q. Covering 284 square miles, where is the world's largest infantry camp located?

A. Fort Benning.

Q. What is the name of the onetime plantation house, tavern, trading post and post office found in Toccoa?

A. Traveler's Rest.

———◆———

Q. In what Atlanta neighborhood would you find the Governor's Mansion?

A. Buckhead.

———◆———

Q. Burke, Camden, Chatham, Effingham, Glynn, Liberty, Richmond and Wilkes counties, formed in 1777, are known by what name?

A. Constitutional Counties.

———◆———

Q. What is the highest elevation in the state?

A. 4,784 feet above sea level, Brasstown Bald Mountain.

———◆———

Q. Where does Atlanta's International rank among the world's busiest airports?

A. Second, Chicago's O'Hare being first.

———◆———

Q. For whose French estate was LaGrange named?

A. Marquis de LaFayette.

———◆———

Q. What is the largest religious group in the state?

A. Baptist.

Q. Where did Eli Whitney establish his first ginnery?

A. Smyrna in Wilkes County.

———◆———

Q. The Lewis B. Wilson Airport in Macon was first known by what name?

A. Cochran Field.

———◆———

Q. What is the perimeter mileage of the state?

A. 1,051 miles.

———◆———

Q. Where is the Doll Gallery, featuring over 1,500 dolls, situated?

A. Kennesaw.

———◆———

Q. The B. F. Goodrich Company established what town in Upham County in 1929 and annexed into Thomaston in 1958?

A. Silverton.

———◆———

Q. In 1971 the Modern States Life Insurance Company purchased what 3,200-foot-high mountain in Rabun County?

A. Screamer Mountain.

———◆———

Q. What community is known as "The Crossroads of Georgia" due to its being very close to the geographic center of the state?

A. Perry.

Q. From what Georgia county were Treutlen, Laurens, Johnson, Telfair, Dodge, Jenkins, Emanuel, Bulloch, Tatnall, Toombs and Wheeler counties taken?

A. Montgomery County.

————◆————

Q. Ellen Louise Axson married Woodrow Wilson in 1885 in what Georgia city?

A. Savannah.

————◆————

Q. Which community is known as the "Carpet Capital of the World"?

A. Dalton.

————◆————

Q. What is the county seat of Chattooga County?

A. Summerville.

————◆————

Q. The State of Georgia purchased Jekyll Island in what year?

A. 1947.

————◆————

Q. Henry B. Holliday, father of notorious western gunman John Henry "Doc" Holliday, served as the first court clerk in which county?

A. Spalding County.

————◆————

Q. Which community is noted for its world famous, old-fashioned fruit cakes?

A. Claxton, Claxton Bakery, Inc.

Q. The county line between Johnson and Emanuel counties forms a large "Z" through which community?

A. Adrian.

◆

Q. What was the only college for men that remained open during the Civil War?

A. Mercer University.

◆

Q. Moody Air Force Base in Lowndes-Lanier counties is named after what man?

A. George Putnam Moody, a graduate of West Point.

◆

Q. Which city is known as "Fountain City"?
A. Columbus.

◆

Q. Mule Camp Springs was the early name for what present day community?

A. Gainesville.

◆

Q. Erected in 1861, the last remaining Confederate flagpole is situated in what community?

A. Blakely.

◆

Q. What state park, situated on the shore of Lake Blackshear in Crisp County, is named in honor of men and women from the state who served in World Wars I and II?

A. Georgia Veterans Memorial State Park.

Q. Blakely is known by what nickname?

A. "Peanut Capital of the World."

———◆———

Q. To what did Berlin in Colquitt County change its name temporarily during World War I?

A. Lens.

———◆———

Q. When was the nickname "Gate City" first applied to Atlanta?

A. 1857, in a toast at a banquet given in Charleston, South Carolina.

———◆———

Q. What is the meaning of the term *piedmont*, which is applied to the region of the state between the Appalachians and the coastal plains?

A. Foot hills.

———◆———

Q. What is the name of the restored 1836 stagecoach inn located in Lumpkin?

A. Bedingfield Inn.

———◆———

Q. How many acres are included in the Chattahoochee National Forest?

A. 739,252 acres.

———◆———

Q. What two cities are connected by the Jim L. Gillis Highway, I-16?

A. Macon and Savannah.

Q. Where was the first black Moslem sect established in the state?

A. Augusta.

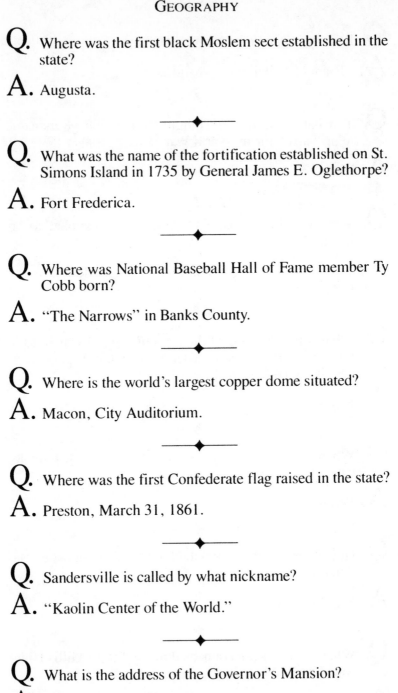

Q. What was the name of the fortification established on St. Simons Island in 1735 by General James E. Oglethorpe?

A. Fort Frederica.

Q. Where was National Baseball Hall of Fame member Ty Cobb born?

A. "The Narrows" in Banks County.

Q. Where is the world's largest copper dome situated?

A. Macon, City Auditorium.

Q. Where was the first Confederate flag raised in the state?

A. Preston, March 31, 1861.

Q. Sandersville is called by what nickname?

A. "Kaolin Center of the World."

Q. What is the address of the Governor's Mansion?

A. 391 W. Paces Ferry Road NW, Atlanta.

Q. What is the largest undeveloped island on the Atlantic Coast?

A. Cumberland Island.

Q. Mountain View in Clay County was originally known by what name?

A. Rough and Ready.

Q. Who owned several plantations on Ford Island in the Ogeechee River?

A. Henry Ford.

Q. Counties in the state of Georgia are subdivided into political divisions known by what name?

A. Militia districts.

Q. Where was American civil rights leader Martin Luther King, Jr. born?

A. Atlanta.

Q. Where in the state is the oldest congregation in the United States practicing Reform Judaism?

A. Savannah, Mickvi Israel Temple.

Q. This upper tributary of Hannahatchee Creek, located in Stewart County, was given what name by surveyor John G. Scruggs on December 25, 1825?

A. Christmas Branch.

Q. The geographic center of the state is located ¼ mile southeast of the junction of Turvin and Savage Creeks in what county?

A. Twiggs County.

———◆———

Q. Where are former governors James Milton Smith, 1872—1877, and Allen Daniel Candler, 1898—1902, buried?

A. Alta Vista Cemetery in Gainesville.

———◆———

Q. The largest computer-controlled railroad classification yard in North America is located in what community?

A. Waycross.

———◆———

Q. What was the actual name of the Confederate prison camp at Andersonville?

A. Camp Sumpter.

———◆———

Q. What two lakes does Georgia share with the neighboring state of South Carolina?

A. Hartwell and Clark Hill lakes.

———◆———

Q. Where can the "largest peanut in the world" be seen?

A. Ashburn.

———◆———

Q. Dade County occupies which corner of the state?

A. Northwest corner.

Q. Where does Georgia rank in size compared to all other states?

A. 21st in size.

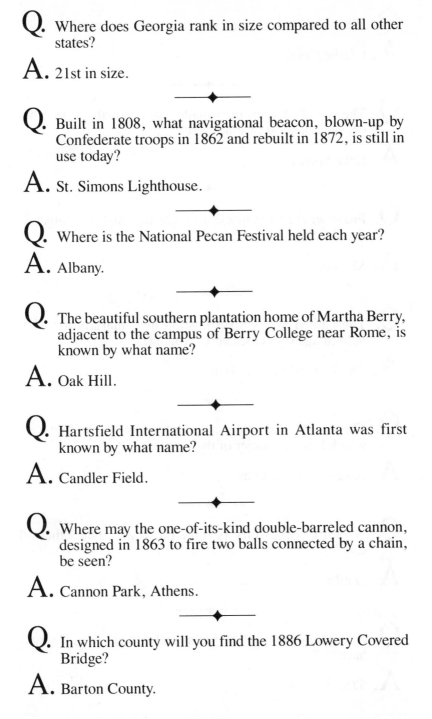

Q. Built in 1808, what navigational beacon, blown-up by Confederate troops in 1862 and rebuilt in 1872, is still in use today?

A. St. Simons Lighthouse.

Q. Where is the National Pecan Festival held each year?

A. Albany.

Q. The beautiful southern plantation home of Martha Berry, adjacent to the campus of Berry College near Rome, is known by what name?

A. Oak Hill.

Q. Hartsfield International Airport in Atlanta was first known by what name?

A. Candler Field.

Q. Where may the one-of-its-kind double-barreled cannon, designed in 1863 to fire two balls connected by a chain, be seen?

A. Cannon Park, Athens.

Q. In which county will you find the 1886 Lowery Covered Bridge?

A. Barton County.

Q. What is the smallest county in area in the state?

A. Clarke County.

Q. The world's largest man-made beach is claimed by what private lake east of Jonesboro?

A. Lake Spivey.

Q. From where were bricks brought to construct Albany's first brick house in 1860?

A. Macon.

Q. The United States Sixth District headquarters for what federal agency is located in Atlanta?

A. The Federal Reserve Bank.

Q. The county seat of Jones County is named in honor of which large financier of the Confederacy?

A. James Madison Gray.

Q. Which Georgia city is referred to as "The Emerald City"?

A. Dublin.

Q. About how many cities, towns and villages does Georgia have?

A. 575.

Q. Where is the University of Georgia located?

A. Athens.

———◆———

Q. For whom was Georgia named?

A. King George II of England.

———◆———

Q. What Decatur County town is named in honor of the naval officer who commanded the *U. S. Constitution*?

A. Bainbridge, in honor of William Bainbridge.

———◆———

Q. Where did President Franklin D. Roosevelt establish his Little White House?

A. Warm Springs.

———◆———

Q. What Georgia community is known as "the city of homes"?

A. Newnan.

———◆———

Q. In which town is the Sorghum Festival held?

A. Blairsville.

———◆———

Q. Waycross is the home of a huge railcar repair facility for which railroad line?

A. Seaboard Coastline Railroad.

Q. The famous Calloway Gardens resort is located in what county?

A. Harris County.

◆

Q. What was the peak percentage of black population reached in the state in 1880?

A. 47 per cent.

◆

Q. What facility in Americus housed thousands of Confederate soldiers as patients between August and December of 1864?

A. Foard Hospital.

◆

Q. Has the Georgia General Assembly ever designated an official state nickname?

A. No.

◆

Q. In Cornelia, what honors the area's apple growing industry?

A. The Big Red Apple Monument.

◆

Q. Near which town is the Old Wooden Jail located in which Aaron Burr was incarcerated in 1807 while en route to Virginia to stand trial for treason?

A. Sandersville.

◆

Q. What port city is known as the shrimp capital of the world?

A. Brunswick.

Q. What community in Echols County received its name from some critical customers of a general store about the merchandise provided?

A. Needmore.

———◆———

Q. Where in Georgia did the infamous "Trail of Tears" begin for the relocation of the Cherokee Indians to western territories?

A. Red Clay.

———◆———

Q. Who became governor of the state in 1983?

A. Joe Frank Harris.

———◆———

Q. How does Georgia rank in land area when compared with the other states east of the Mississippi River?

A. Largest.

———◆———

Q. What is the largest lake in Rabun County?

A. Lake Burton.

———◆———

Q. For what company was the community of Enterprise in Morgan County named?

A. Enterprise Compress Company of Augusta.

———◆———

Q. Who was the Atlanta dentist and Confederate Army officer for whom Hapeville in Fulton County is named?

A. Dr. Samuel Hape.

Q. What Jenkins County community was named for the heroic captain of the *S. S. Central America* who went down with his ship on September 12, 1856, after seeing to the safety of the women and children passengers?

A. Herndon, named for Captain William Lewis Herndon.

———◆———

Q. Where is the home of the Georgia Mountain Fair?

A. Hiwassee.

———◆———

Q. For whom was Buchanan County named?

A. James Buchanan, fifteenth President of the United States.

———◆———

Q. What is Rabun County's single largest industry?

A. Tourism.

———◆———

Q. Which Houston County town is called "The Motel City"?

A. Perry.

———◆———

Q. What first attracted early pioneers to settle Columbus?

A. The Chattahoochee River and its falls.

———◆———

Q. In what city is the Andrew Low House, home of Juliette Gordon Low, Girl Scout founder, located?

A. Savannah.

Q. Originally known as Puddleville, this Cook County community changed its name to Adel in 1889 by picking out the four middle letters of what Pennsylvania city?

A. Philadelphia.

———◆———

Q. What is the state motto of Georgia?

A. Wisdom, Justice and Moderation.

———◆———

Q. Which town is called the "Watermelon Capital of the World"?

A. Cordele.

———◆———

Q. Georgia has how many United States senators?

A. Two.

———◆———

Q. Where is Mule Day held each fall?

A. Calvary.

———◆———

Q. How high is the central mound at the famous Etowah Mound complex near Cartersville?

A. 65 feet high.

———◆———

Q. What United States military reservation was closed in 1947, only to have a town of the same name incorporated in the same area two years later?

A. Fort Oglethorpe.

Q. Where were live oak timbers cut for use in the construction of the Brooklyn Bridge?

A. Gascoigne Bluff, St. Simons.

Q. What is the greatest distance east to west in the state?
A. 250 miles.

Q. Where was the birthplace of Benjamin Harvey Hill, considered to be Jefferson Davis' ablest supporter?

A. Near Hillsboro.

Q. Until 1942, which county could only be entered by way of Alabama or Tennessee?

A. Dade County.

Q. Chickamauga in Walker County was first known by what name?

A. Crawfish Spring.

Q. An early name of Dahlonega was the same as what country?

A. Mexico.

Q. Rutledge is located near which state park?
A. Hard Labor Creek State Park.

Q. The Kolomoki Mounds State Park is located in which county?

A. Early County.

Q. What is the county seat of Brooks County?

A. Quitman.

Q. What is the name of the Civil War cannon manufacuturers whose buildings have been renovated into Columbus' Convention and Trade Center?

A. Columbus Iron Works.

Q. How many United States representatives does Georgia have?

A. Ten.

Q. Where does the southern end of the Appalachian Trail terminate?

A. Springer Mountain.

Q. What do the initials of the FDR school site, located in Seminole County, stand for?

A. The consolidated schools of Fairchild, Desser and Reynoldsville.

Q. Stone Mountain was named on December 24, 1847, but previous to that it was incorporated under what name?

A. New Gibralter.

Q. Fort Augusta was known by what name during the Revolutionary War?

A. Fort Cornwallis.

———◆———

Q. Brunswick is recognized as a world center for what type of processed food dishes?

A. Seafood dishes.

———◆———

Q. American novelist Carson McCullers was born in what Georgia city?

A. Columbus.

———◆———

Q. The name for Hannahatchee Creek in Stewart County is based on what two Muskhogean Indian words?

A. *Achina*, meaning cedar; *hachi*, meaning creek.

———◆———

Q. What was the name of the 10,000 acre estate established in Bartow County just prior to the Civil War by the then wealthiest man in Savannah?

A. Barnsley Gardens.

———◆———

Q. How many senators are there within the state legislature?

A. 56.

———◆———

Q. In 1868, what city became the capital of the newly reorganized State of Georgia?

A. Atlanta.

Q. What small community, originally known as Wellston, grew to be Georgia's 8th largest city in 42 short years?

A. Warner Robins.

Q. Located at Oxford, Oxford College is a branch of what university?

A. Emory University.

Q. "The Jonquil City" is the nickname of what town?

A. Smyrna.

Q. The name *Plains* is the shortened form of the name of what older community located about one mile north of the town's present location?

A. Plains of Dura.

Q. Where was the last significant land battle of the War Between the States fought?

A. Columbus, April 16, 1865.

Q. Which town refers to itself as the "Poultry Capital of the World?

A. Gainesville.

Q. Who serves as president of the Martin Luther King, Jr. Center for Social Change in Atlanta?

A. Coretta Scott King.

Q. What was the name given to the refugee and relocation camp set up by Governor Joseph E. Brown in Dawson following the fall of Atlanta in 1864?

A. Exile Camp.

———◆———

Q. Which town has the most southeasterly location in the state?

A. St. Marys.

———◆———

Q. What was the name of the 2,170 acre plantation the legislature of Georgia conferred upon Revolutionary War hero Major Nathanael Greene?

A. Mulberry Grove.

———◆———

Q. Adamsville, which has been absorbed by Atlanta, was originally known by what name?

A. Lick Skillet.

———◆———

Q. How many electoral votes does Georgia have?

A. 12.

———◆———

Q. Which county is known as the "Empire County of the Empire State of the South"?

A. Crisp County.

———◆———

Q. How did Newborn, located in Newton County, receive its name?

A. Inhabitants wanted their town "born anew" after hearing sermons from the famous evangelist Sam P. Jones.

ENTERTAINMENT

C H A P T E R   T W O

Q. Six Flags Over Georgia covers how many acres?

A. 331 acres.

---◆---

Q. In which community is the Million Pines Festival held?

A. Soperton.

---◆---

Q. What famous gospel music quartet worked out of Atlanta from 1948 until 1974?

A. The Statesmen with Hovie Lister.

---◆---

Q. Atlanta-born actor DeForrest Kelley gained fame playing what character in the *Star Trek* series?

A. Dr. McCoy.

---◆---

Q. What movie filmed in Georgia takes an imprisoned football star and turns him into a coach of the prison football team?

A. *The Longest Yard*, 1974.

Q. What Georgia-born multi-talented performer hit the Top 40 national charts in 1961 with *Jeremiah Peabody's Poly-unsaturated, Quick-dissolving, Fast-acting, Pleasant-tasting Green and Purple Pills?*

A. Ray Stevens.

———◆———

Q. What festival is held in early April in Sylvania?

A. The Livestock Festival.

———◆———

Q. What television movie starring June Carter Cash, Johnny Cash and Andy Griffith took place in one of the state's western counties?

A. *Murder in Coweta County.*

———◆———

Q. Who is the Liveoak Gardens-born singer, instrumentalist and songwriter who won over Greenwich Village audiences with his unique country folk music in the mid-1960s?

A. Patrick "Pat" Sky.

———◆———

Q. What is the name of the 1,500-acre amusement resort area located near Douglas that features the Jet Star Coaster?

A. Holiday Beach.

———◆———

Q. Who is the Macon-born vocalist noted for her passionate southern soul music?

A. Randy Crawford.

———◆———

Q. Who was the nationally famous toothless, raspy-voiced, black comedienne who was born in Brevard in 1897?

A. Moms Mabley.

Q. What television personality born in Nelson is best known for starring in *Movin On,* 1974—1976, *B. J. and the Bear,* 1979, and *Sheriff Lobo,* 1979—1981?

A. Claude Akins.

Q. What record won Albany-born Ray Charles two Grammy Awards in 1966 for best rhythm and blues?

A. *Crying Time.*

Q. From 1973 through 1985, how many motion pictures, television films and specials were shot in Georgia?

A. 218.

Q. What group of musicians toured the state following the War Between the States to raise money for Confederate soldiers?

A. The Atlanta Amateurs.

Q. What is the flagship station for cable giant Turner Communications?

A. WTCG-TV, Channel 17, Atlanta.

Q. The country music performing Forrester Sisters are from what Georgia community?

A. Stone Mountain.

Q. What country music singer, guitarist and songwriter was born on June 8, 1932 in Tennga?

A. Clyde Beavers.

Q. What drive-in, located in Atlanta, has the distinction of being the largest in the world?

A. The Varsity.

———◆———

Q. *Roots*, filmed for television in part in and around Savannah, was a dramatization based on the book by what author?

A. Alex Hailey.

———◆———

Q. What Easter festivity is held on Jekyll Island?

A. The Great Golden Easter Egg Hunt.

———◆———

Q. What professional football player turned actor was born on St. Simons Island and appeared in such films as *The Dirty Dozen*, 1967, *I Escaped from Devil's Island*, 1973, and *One Down, Two to Go*, 1982?

A. Jim Brown.

———◆———

Q. Noted female country and western bassist and songwriter Kitty Wilson was born in which Georgia town?

A. Rome.

———◆———

Q. Where was Otis Redding born on September 9, 1941?

A. Dawson.

———◆———

Q. What Atlanta outdoor ampitheater hosts events from May through September featuring the Symphony, jazz concerts and popular performers such as James Brown and Dionne Warwick?

A. Chastain Park.

Q. Who from Canton helped pioneer television commercial jingles with tunes for hair care products like *Wildroot Cream Oil* and *White Rain Shampoo*?

A. Lee Roy Abernathy.

———◆———

Q. How many episodes of the *Dukes of Hazzard* were shot in Georgia in 1979?

A. Five episodes.

———◆———

Q. Neva Jane Langley won what title while representing Georgia in 1953?

A. Miss America.

———◆———

Q. What was James Brown's first record release?

A. *Please, Please, Please*, 1956.

———◆———

Q. What actor, born in Waycross in 1891, was married to actress Esther Howard and appeared in *The Argyle Case*?

A. Arthur W. Albertson.

———◆———

Q. What southern action drama, shot in Georgia, starred Burt Reynolds and was a sequel to *White Lightning*?

A. *Gator*.

———◆———

Q. What innovative station break technique was introduced by WSB radio, Atlanta?

A. The use of musical station identification call letters.

Q. What jazz and blues singer born in Cordele was a blues singer in Count Basie's Orchestra from 1954—1961?

A. Joe Williams.

———◆———

Q. The character "Adam" on *Bonanza* was played by what Waycross-born actor?

A. Pernell Roberts.

———◆———

Q. Filmed entirely in central Georgia, what TV movie was a dramatization of the 1931 civil rights case involving nine Alabama black men accused of raping two white women?

A. *Judge Horton and the Scottsboro Boys.*

———◆———

Q. What is distinctive about the Scream Machine at Six Flags Over Georgia?

A. It is the longest and tallest wooden roller coaster in the world.

———◆———

Q. Where was Grand Ole Opry member Roy Drusky born on June 22, 1930?

A. Atlanta.

———◆———

Q. Ellijay is the site of which fall festival?

A. The Apple Festival.

———◆———

Q. What soap opera filmed segments of its show in Georgia in 1981?

A. *All My Children.*

Q. In the early 1940s, what gospel group was sponsored on the radio in Atlanta by the SunCrest Bottling Company?

A. The LeFevres.

———◆———

Q. Black actress/director Osceola Archer was born in what Georgia city?

A. Albany.

———◆———

Q. What amusement park is located near Rossville?

A. Lake Winnepesaukah Amusement Park.

———◆———

Q. What Albany-born trumpet player and band leader gained national fame while playing two years for Benny Goodman?

A. Harry Haag James.

———◆———

Q. Where can you see Elvis Presley's first limousine?

A. Vintage Auto Museum, Dillard.

———◆———

Q. What group did Atlanta-born jazz musician Edgar W. "Puddinghead" Battle form at the age of 15?

A. The Dixie Serenaders at Morris Brown University.

———◆———

Q. What drama about the illegal sport of cockfighting was filmed in Georgia in 1974 starring Warren Oates?

A. *Cockfighter.*

Q. What comedy/variety special about great American trains was filmed partly in Georgia and aired on television in 1974?

A. *Johnny Cash Ridin' the Rails.*

———◆———

Q. When did the South's first television station, WSB-TV Atlanta, begin operation?

A. 1948.

———◆———

Q. Georgia-born Ray Stevens won a Grammy Award in 1970 for male pop vocalist with what song?

A. *Everything Is Beautiful.*

———◆———

Q. What black actor born in Sanderville appeared during the 1970s on such television shows as *The Partridge Family, Marcus Welby, M. D., Streets of San Francisco* and *Columbo*?

A. Herbert Jefferson, Jr.

———◆———

Q. *Scared to Death*, a 1980 film partially produced in Georgia, featured what synthesized genetic organism as the villain creature?

A. *Syngenor.*

———◆———

Q. What festival celebrates the original European Saint Nicholas Eve?

A. The Sugarplum Festival at Stone Mountain Village.

———◆———

Q. What recording artist born in Atlanta received three gold records for *I'm Sorry, Rocking Around the Christmas Tree*, and *All Alone Am I*?

A. Brenda Lee.

Q. What Fort Benning-born actress appeared in several movies, including *A Shot in the Dark, Dr. Strangelove, Casino Royale, Hammerhead* and *Car Wash*?

A. Tracy Reed.

———◆———

Q. What was Moms Mabley's actual name?

A. Loretta Mary Aiken.

———◆———

Q. What is the Whitfield County community that hosts the Old Time Fiddlin' Convention each August?

A. Dalton.

———◆———

Q. Who directed *Gone With the Wind*?

A. Victor Fleming.

———◆———

Q. What town was the birthplace of actress Joanne Woodward?

A. Thomasville.

———◆———

Q. What musician, composer and singer born in Atlanta has many hit records including *When You're Hot, You're Hot*?

A. Jerry Reed.

———◆———

Q. The world's only triple loop roller coaster, located at Six Flags Over Georgia, is known by what name?

A. The Mind Bender.

Q. What group had a smash hit in 1973 with its recording of *Midnight Train to Georgia?*

A. Gladys Knight and the Pips.

———◆———

Q. Where was country western bandleader Gid Tanner born in 1885?

A. Near Monroe.

———◆———

Q. The adventures of a black baseball team in the 1940s is portrayed in what Universal film shot in the state?

A. *The Bingo Long Traveling All-Stars and Motor Kings*, 1975—1976.

———◆———

Q. Claudia Coleman, screen, stage and vaudeville actress of the 1930s, was born in 1889 in what city?

A. Atlanta.

———◆———

Q. What was the name of Roy Drusky's first hit record on the Starday label in 1953?

A. *Such a Fool.*

———◆———

Q. What recording by Dawson-born Otis Redding became number one in the United States and number three in the United Kingdom?

A. *Sittin' on the Dock of the Bay.*

———◆———

Q. Which beloved Georgia-born actor, comedian and recording artist appeared in numerous commercials and is best known for being the voice of Walt Disney's Winnie the Pooh and the narrator of *Jungle Book?*

A. Sterling Holloway.

Q. What was the name of Pete Drake's group that worked out of Atlanta in the mid and late 1950s?

A. Sons of the South.

———◆———

Q. What made-for-television miniseries was filmed in Georgia in 1974 to help celebrate the Bicentennial?

A. *Give Me Liberty.*

———◆———

Q. The Gold Leaf Festival may be enjoyed each August in what community?

A. Pelham.

———◆———

Q. Who is the Athens-born guitar player who won five consecutive awards for "Best Acoustic Guitarist" from *Guitar Player* magazine?

A. Leo Kottke.

———◆———

Q. What type of programming was pioneered by Turner Broadcasting on June 1, 1980?

A. Twenty-four-hour-a-day all news for cable television.

———◆———

Q. Where was James Brown born?

A. Augusta, May 3, 1933.

———◆———

Q. What stage, screen and television actor born in Georgia appeared in *The Life of Riley*, 1949; *The Bad and the Beautiful*, 1952; and *Lolita*, 1962?

A. William E. Greene.

Q. How long was the movie version of *Gone With the Wind*?

A. 220 minutes.

———◆———

Q. Ray Charles, musician, singer and composer, was born in what city?

A. Albany.

———◆———

Q. What black actor born in Tifton appeared in such "soaps" as *All My Children, Search for Tomorrow* and *Guiding Light?*

A. Dino Shorte.

———◆———

Q. What Monroe-born trumpet player is best known for his work with Charles Mingus?

A. Lonnie Hillyer.

———◆———

Q. In 1980, a portion of what movie starring Kurt Russell in the character of Snake Plissken was shot in Georgia?

A. *Escape from New York.*

———◆———

Q. What Georgia-born baseball star appeared in *Somewhere in Georgia*, 1916; *The Ninth Inning*, 1942; and *Angels in the Outfield*, 1951?

A. Ty Cobb.

———◆———

Q. Lou McGarity, trombonist and singer who toured with Bob Crosby in 1964 and in 1967 became a charter member of the World's Greatest Jazz Band, was born in what Georgia community?

A. Athens.

Q. John Schneider auditioned in Atlanta for what television series?

A. *The Dukes of Hazzard.*

———◆———

Q. What Savannah-born screen, stage, radio and television actor has appeared in many motion pictures, including *The More the Merrier*, 1943; *Gentlemen Prefer Blondes*, 1953; and *That's Entertainment*, (film clip) 1974?

A. Charles Douville Coburn.

———◆———

Q. In which month is the Thomasville Rose Festival usually held?

A. April.

———◆———

Q. What well-known actor sometimes lived on Tybee Island?

A. James Coburn.

———◆———

Q. Georgia-born rhythm and blues singer Willie Jackson won what coveted award in 1973?

A. *Cashbox* Best Female Rhythm and Blues Vocalist.

———◆———

Q. What great comedian was born in Harlem, Georgia on January 18, 1892?

A. Oliver Norvell Hardy of Laurel and Hardy fame.

———◆———

Q. Who played the role of Rhett Butler in the movie version of *Gone With the Wind*?

A. Clark Gable.

Q. What Atlanta resident came to fame with such songs as *Ruby, Don't Take Your Love to Town, You Picked a Fine Time to Leave Me Lucille* and *The Gambler?*

A. Kenny Rogers.

———◆———

Q. James Brown was a member of what group when he began his career?

A. The Famous Flames.

———◆———

Q. What is the name of the authentic steam engine excursion railroad line in Hartwell?

A. The Red Carpet Line.

———◆———

Q. What was the first radio station in the South, established by the *Atlanta Journal* in 1922?

A. WSB.

———◆———

Q. What Waycross-born actor became famous as the lead in the television series *Dan August*, 1970—1971?

A. Burt Reynolds.

———◆———

Q. What production for GE Theater, filmed partly in Georgia, was the story of a Detroit family vacationing in the South?

A. *Just an Old Sweet Song*, 1976.

———◆———

Q. The Lewis Family, known nationally as the "First Family of Bluegrass-Gospel Music," hails from what Georgia town?

A. Lincolnton.

Q. What entertainer, born in Atlanta, was master of ceremonies for the Miss America Pageants from 1956—1979?

A. Bert Parks.

Q. What movie was filmed on northeast Georgia's Chattooga River?

A. *Deliverance.*

Q. In 1955, what recording by Georgia-born "Little Richard" became a million copy bestseller?

A. *Tutti Frutti.*

Q. Where is the Marigold Festival held?

A. Winterville.

Q. Macon-born musician Emmett Berry played what instrument with Teddy Wilson, Eddie Heywood and Count Basie in the 1930s?

A. Trumpet.

Q. What musical event first held in 1885 in Atlanta became an annual event?

A. Fiddler's Convention.

Q. Which novel by Erskine Caldwell, born in White Oak, was turned into a Broadway play and ran for more than seven years?

A. *Tobacco Road.*

Q. Actress Gracie Maldell "Georgia" Burke, whose career covered radio, television, movies and theater, was born in 1906 in what town?

A. La Grange.

———◆———

Q. What Walt Disney production was filmed in part in Georgia in 1977?

A. *Million Dollar Dixie Deliverance*.

———◆———

Q. What was the actual name of Ma Rainey, who was born in Columbus in 1886 and is known as the " Mother of the Blues"?

A. Gertrude Malissa Nix Pridgett.

———◆———

Q. What Athens-born actress played pretty-girl roles in *Never Say Never Again*, 1983; and *The Natural*, 1984?

A. Kim Basinger.

———◆———

Q. The annual Heritage Holidays are held in which community?

A. Rome.

———◆———

Q. What film, produced in 1979 and filmed in part in Georgia, is based on a novel by Flannery O'Connor?

A. *Wise Blood*.

———◆———

Q. In what town was the well-known actor Sterling Holloway born?

A. Cedartown.

Q. What famous Savannah composer was widely known for such hits as *Come Rain or Come Shine* and *That Old Black Magic*?

A. Johnny Mercer.

◆

Q. In 1952 what Atlanta-born singer won Ted Mack's Amateur Hour at the age of 8?

A. Gladys Knight.

◆

Q. Known as one of the most original and forceful trombone soloists of the swing era, what jazz artist hailed from Social Circle, Georgia?

A. Jack (J. C.) Higginbotham.

◆

Q. In what year was the movie *Gone With the Wind* released?
A. 1939.

◆

Q. What Savannah-born actor, director, producer and writer is best known for starring in Mickey Spillane's *Mike Hammer* television series?

A. Stacy Keach, Jr.

◆

Q. In what year did Albany-born trumpeteer Harry James form his first band?

A. 1939.

◆

Q. Where in Emanuel County is the Pine Tree Festival held?
A. Swainsboro.

Q. Where was black comedian Nipsey Russell born?

A. Atlanta.

———◆———

Q. The Stovall Covered Bridge, built in 1895 near Helen, was featured in what movie?

A. *I'd Climb the Highest Mountain*.

———◆———

Q. What is the full name of "Little Richard"?

A. Richard Penniman.

———◆———

Q. Which western movie shot in Georgia in 1979, dealing with the famous James and Younger bank raid in Northfield, Minnesota, starred the Carradine and Keach brothers?

A. *The Long Riders*.

———◆———

Q. Where is the country music Top of Georgia Jamboree held?

A. Rabun Gap Elementary School, Dillard.

———◆———

Q. What onetime Atlanta resident was named Best New Male Country Artist in 1983 by the Academy of Country Music?

A. John Schneidner.

———◆———

Q. Georgia's film industry is monitored by which state department?

A. Georgia Department of Industry and Trade.

Q. What is the name of Ray Charles' own record label?

A. Tangerine Records.

Q. Which Academy Award-winning actress lived in the community of Carrollton from the late 60s to the early 70s?

A. Susan Hayward.

Q. Eli Robinson, a veteran of Count Basie's band, was born in which Georgia community?

A. Greenville.

Q. Actor Demond Wilson of *Sanford and Son* fame was born in which southern Georgia town?

A. Valdosta.

Q. Georgia resident Jim Fowler has been the longtime co-host and now host of which television series?

A. Mutual of Omaha's *Wild Kingdom*.

Q. What system did the Federal Communications Commission approve in 1976 for use by Turner Communications?

A. A satellite-relay system.

Q. What revenge-of-nature science fiction film featuring man-eating worms was shot in Georgia in 1975?

A. *Squirm*.

Q. What Georgia-born pro football player in the 1970s made numerous commercials, television guest appearances and appeared in such movies as *In Cold Blood*, *The Liberation of L. B. Jones* and *Skyjacked*?

A. Roosevelt "Rosey" Grier.

———◆———

Q. What was the name of the first successful black musical and comedy troup?

A. The Georgia Minstrels.

———◆———

Q. The Trout Festival is held each spring in which community?

A. Dahlonega.

———◆———

Q. Who starred in the 1981 made-for-television movie, *Coward of the County*, and had a hit recording of the same title?

A. Georgia-born Kenny Rogers.

———◆———

Q. What world's leading exponent of bottleneck slide guitar was killed in a motorcycle accident in Macon in 1971?

A. Duane Allman of the Allman Brothers Band.

———◆———

Q. Which single and album went gold for Joe South in 1969?

A. *Games People Play*.

———◆———

Q. Where was "Little Richard" born?

A. Macon, December 25, 1932.

Q. What Waycross-born musician has toured with such jazz greats as Count Basie, Dizzy Gillespie, Paul Willams and Aretha Franklin?

A. Daniel William (Danny) Moore.

◆

Q. Each May, Brunswick is the site of which festival?

A. The Brunswick Golden Isles Spring Fiesta.

◆

Q. Which Atlanta-born guitarist was propelled into national recognition with his recording of *Talking Steel Guitar*?

A. Pete Drake.

◆

Q. Who starred in *Greased Lightning*, partly filmed in Georgia, the biography of Wendell Scott, the first black stock-car racing driver?

A. Richard Pryor.

◆

Q. What movie set in the fifties portrays two teenagers who pick up a waitress only to find themselves in trouble with a sheriff?

A. *Return to Macon County Line*, 1975.

◆

Q. Where are the fall Oktoberfest and winter Fasching Masquerade Karnival held?

A. Helen.

◆

Q. Cartersville is the birthplace of which noted hootenanny era folk singer?

A. Hedy West.

Q. Known best for his originality on the flute, what Savannah-born composer played with Dizzy Gillespie in the 1940s and early 60s and has toured Europe and the Far East extensively?

A. James Moody.

Q. NBC Night at the Movies presented *The Greatest Gift*, filmed partly in Georgia, as a pilot for *The Family Holvak* series starring what actor as the Rev. Holvak?

A. Glenn Ford.

Q. In what film do three Atlanta workers design a plan to raise money for their church by hypnotizing a boxer into winning a fight?

A. *Let's Do It Again*, 1975.

Q. Country music fiddler Clayton "Pappy" McMichen, born in Allatoona, was noted for forming what Dixieland group?

A. The Georgia Wildcats.

Q. What screen, stage and vaudeville actress, born in Gainesville, appeared in *The Ragamuffin,* 1916?

A. Minnette Barrett.

Q. Which black actor from Georgia appeared in the 1976 movie *Network*?

A. Author N. Burghardt-Banks.

Q. What Savannah-born Louis Armstrong and J. Lunceford soloist appeared on a segment of the TV series *Hawaii Five-O* with Nancy Wilson?

A. James Osborne (Trummy) Young.

Q. When did James Brown receive his first Grammy Award?

A. 1965.

———◆———

Q. The Burt Reynolds movie, *Smokey and the Bandit*, which was partially filmed in Georgia, starred what actor in the role of Sheriff Buford T. Justice?

A. Jackie Gleason.

———◆———

Q. Born in Marietta in 1941, Priscilla Mitchell had what number one country duet hit with Roy Drusky in 1965?

A. *Yes, Mr. Peters.*

———◆———

Q. What guitar sessions-man, born in Atlanta on February 28, 1942, went on to become a star in his own right?

A. Joe South.

———◆———

Q. What actor/author born in Cogdell wrote *Escape to Freedom: The Story of Young Frederick Douglass*, in 1978?

A. Ossie Davis.

———◆———

Q. What former Duke Ellington and Charlie Johnson trumpet star was born in Claxton?

A. Cladys (Jabbo) Smith.

———◆———

Q. What pseudonym did Priscilla Mitchell use for her rock n' roll recordings on the Smash label in the mid-1960s?

A. Sadina.

Q. What Atlanta-born actor appeared in several movies, including *Fingerprints Don't Lie*, *Gene Autry and the Mounties* and *Texans Never Cry*, all in 1951?

A. Royal (Roy) Butler.

Q. Gladys Knight's brother and two cousins formed what musical support group for her?

A. The Pips.

Q. What was the name of Gid Tanner's early country music group that worked out of Atlanta in the mid-1920s?

A. The Skillet Lickers.

Q. Which Savannah-born jazz banjo and guitar player worked with such greats as Jelly Roll Morton and Louis Armstrong in the 1920s and 1930s?

A. Lee L. Blair.

Q. Where was black actress Pauline Evelyn Myers, who appared in *Green Pasture*, *Tarzan's Flight for Life*, *Tick...Tick...Tick* and *Lady Sings the Blues*, born?

A. Ocilla.

Q. Who was chosen in 1910 to be the municipal organist of Atlanta?

A. Percy Starnes.

Q. What Covington-born tenor sax player began his career in Georgia and played behind Sam Cooke and Hank Ballard in Atlanta?

A. George Rufus Adams.

HISTORY

Q. What two young Anglican clergymen came to Georgia in 1836 and later founded Methodism?

A. John and Charles Wesley.

———◆———

Q. When were the last Cherokee Indians removed from Georgia?

A. 1838.

———◆———

Q. Jimmy Carter served as President of the United States during what years?

A. 1977—1981.

———◆———

Q. What was the date of the first national holiday in honor of the birthday of Dr. Martin Luther King, Jr.?

A. Monday, January 20, 1986.

———◆———

Q. When did Georgia become a state?

A. January 2, 1788.

Q. Ft. Benning, adjoining Columbus, is named for what distinguished Confederate General?

A. Native son Henry L. Benning.

Q. What was the first nuclear powered merchant vessel?

A. The *N S Savannah*.

Q. What highly decorated air ace of World Wars I and II was a native of Savannah?

A. Major General Frank O'Driscoll Hunter.

Q. Which county is named for the first president of the Central of Georgia Railroad?

A. Gordon County, for William Washington Gordon.

Q. In what year were women first allowed to practice law in the courts of Georgia?

A. 1915.

Q. What religious group was excluded from the Colony of Georgia for fear that its members would spy for the French in Louisiana and the Spanish in Florida?

A. The Roman Catholics.

Q. Who, born in Cherokee County, served as Secretary of State from 1961 to 1969 under Presidents John F. Kennedy and Lyndon B. Johnson?

A. Dean Rusk.

Q. How many machinists in Atlanta formed the first machinist's union in the United States in 1888?

A. 19.

————◆————

Q. Who was the daring French sailor who explored the coast of Georgia in 1562, seeking to establish a colony of French Huguenots?

A. Jean Ribault.

————◆————

Q. In 1943 Georgia was the first state to give 18-year-olds what privilege?

A. The right to vote.

————◆————

Q. In the early years of Georgia colonization the manufacturing and sale of what beverage was prohibited?

A. Whiskey (law repealed in 1742).

————◆————

Q. What was the name of the combined school and orphanage established near Savannah in 1740 that became the most successful charitable and educational endeavor of the colonial period?

A. Bethesda Orphan Home.

————◆————

Q. How much money disappeared from the Confederate treasury in Washington, never to be recovered?

A. 400,000 dollars in gold.

————◆————

Q. Who was the first European to explore Georgia?

A. Hernando de Soto, 1540.

Q. The remains of what two Confederate gunboats are on display at the Confederate Naval Museum in Columbus?

A. The *CSS Chattahoochee* and the *CSS Jackson/ Muscogee.*

———◆———

Q. Cotton production increased from 1,000 bales in 1791 to how many bales in 1860?

A. 701,000.

———◆———

Q. What is the name of the site of the Civil War battle that opened the way to Atlanta for Sherman?

A. Resaca.

———◆———

Q. Who was General James Edward Oglethorpe's half-breed interpreter?

A. Mary Musgrove.

———◆———

Q. As the Confederacy began to crumble, to whom did Georgia surrender its armies?

A. General James H. Wilson.

———◆———

Q. What was the purpose of the expedition organized in 1559 by Luis de Velasco up the Chattahoochee River into northern Georgia?

A. To establish gold mining operations.

———◆———

Q. Born near Augusta, what American soldier commanded American forces during the Spanish-American War and in the Philippine Insurrection of 1900?

A. Joseph Wheeler.

Q. Where was President Franklin D. Roosevelt when he died?

A. The Little White House, Warm Springs.

———◆———

Q. What was the name of the organization that first appeared in the state in 1867 to organize black voters?

A. The Loyal or Union League.

———◆———

Q. What is Georgia's oldest independent (non-tax supported) institution of higher education?

A. LaGrange College.

———◆———

Q. What store has been in continuous operation since 1892 as a general merchandise and farm supply business in Harris County?

A. The Kimbrough Brothers General Store.

———◆———

Q. When did the first 125 colonists arrive in Georgia, under the leadership of James Oglethorpe?

A. February 12, 1733.

———◆———

Q. Where did the Presbyterian Church establish Oglethorpe College in 1836?

A. Near Milledgeville.

———◆———

Q. What religious entity was formed in Augusta in May, 1845, by seceding from the American Baptist Union over, among other issues, slavery?

A. The Southern Baptist Convention.

Q. Georgia, Kentucky and Tennessee are all states claiming to be the birthplace of what famous frontiersman?

A. James Bowie.

———◆———

Q. Where did Pedro Menendez de Aviles establish a Spanish garrison in 1566?

A. St. Catherines Island.

———◆———

Q. What religious group established a mission school for Indians at Irene in 1736?

A. The Moravians.

———◆———

Q. What exclusive boarding house in Atlanta in the early 1900s provided young men of considerable means a name in society?

A. The Bell House (Bell House "boys").

———◆———

Q. What property was stolen from the Presbyterian Church in Madison during the War Between the States, later to be returned by Federal orders?

A. The church's silver communion service.

———◆———

Q. What year did the Jekyll Island Club close?

A. 1942, at the outbreak of World War II.

———◆———

Q. What was the name of the first iron sea vessel, built in Savannah?

A. The *John Randolph,* 1834.

Q. What barbecued delicacy was served President-elect William Howard Taft during his visit to Atlanta in 1909 of which he took only one bite?

A. A thirty-pound 'possum.

Q. Who was the first woman senator of Georgia, who served only one day?

A. Rebecca L. Felton.

Q. How many black members were seated in the state legislature for the first time in 1868?

A. 32 members, 29 representatives and 3 senators.

Q. What powered the paddles of the *Genius of Georgia*, an 1820 Savannah riverboat?

A. Nineteen horses treading on an endless belt.

Q. What speed did the first steamboat built in Georgia attain on the Savannah River?

A. Five miles per hour.

Q. What percentage of Georgia's material wealth was lost due to the Civil War?

A. 75 per cent.

Q. Who was Georgia's last Republican governor?

A. Benjamin Conley, 1871—1872.

Q. Who was the modest young Spanish-American War hero from Marietta who served as Admiral Dewey's flag officer at the Battle of Manila?

A. Lieutenant Thomas M. Brumby.

◆

Q. Which was the last Confederate fort to fall?

A. Fort Tyler, Troup County, April 16, 1865.

◆

Q. In what year was telephone service inaugurated in Atlanta?

A. 1879, with 55 subscribers.

◆

Q. Who built Fort Deposit in Dawson County in 1818 primarily as a food and supplies depot?

A. Andrew Jackson.

◆

Q. Which city was known at one time as the smallest American city with a streetcar system?

A. Valdosta.

◆

Q. What Confederate prison site, located near Millen, was abandoned in December of 1864, only two months after completion?

A. Magnolia Springs.

◆

Q. Numerically, which President of the United States was Jimmy Carter?

A. Thirty-ninth.

Q. When was the capitol building dedicated in Atlanta?

A. July 4, 1889.

◆

Q. How many emigrants arrived in Georgia between 1732 and 1740?

A. 2,500.

◆

Q. The United States Congress authorized the minting of a commemorative half dollar in connection with what Georgia War Between the States memorial project?

A. The Stone Mountain Memorial, 1925.

◆

Q. Under whose leadership did the Ku Klux Klan begin to operate in the state in the spring of 1868?

A. General John B. Gordon.

◆

Q. Where in Wilkes County was the Confederate Cabinet dissolved and the southern army disbanded?

A. Washington.

◆

Q. In what year did Georgia establish its first public school system?

A. 1870.

◆

Q. Who accompanied the original settlers and became the first teacher in the colony of Georgia?

A. Reverend Benjamin Ingham.

Q. Whose election as mayor of Atlanta in 1973 made him the first black mayor of a major southern city?

A. Maynard H. Jackson, Jr.

Q. What world famous aviator visited Southern Airfield in Americus in 1923 to purchase and fly solo a "Jenny" airplane?

A. Charles A. Lindbergh.

Q. What means of mass transit was established in Atlanta in 1871?

A. Horse-drawn streetcars.

Q. What United States legislation was enacted due to the efforts of Georgia to overturn a 1793 Supreme Court ruling allowing individuals to sue states?

A. The Eleventh Amendment to the United States Constitution, 1798.

Q. In 1804, what town became the site of the state capital?

A. Milledgeville.

Q. Where in Georgia did Lutheran emigrants establish two schools in 1734, in which German was the principal language for more than fifty years?

A. Ebenezar.

Q. What year was Coca-Cola first made?

A. 1886.

Q. The Fife House in Fayetteville housed the Fayetteville Academy from 1855 to 1857, attended by which fictional character in *Gone With the Wind*?

A. Scarlett O'Hara.

———◆———

Q. Who built the first steamboat in Georgia in 1807, shortly after Robert Fulton's *Clermont* had been launched?

A. William Longstreet of Augusta.

———◆———

Q. Georgia became the first state to extend what rights to married women?

A. Full property rights, 1866.

———◆———

Q. When did Georgia secede from the Union?

A. January 19, 1861.

———◆———

Q. For what was the penitentiary at Milledgeville utilized during the War Between the States?

A. An armory.

———◆———

Q. What was the first state-owned railroad in the United States created by the Georgia General Assembly on December 21, 1836?

A. The Western and Atlantic Railroad.

———◆———

Q. In 1893 Thomas E. Watson introduced a bill in the United States Congress that created which public service?

A. Rural free mail delivery.

Q. Which educator became well-known for establishing schools for poor Southern mountain people?

A. Martha Berry.

———◆———

Q. Where was the first Negro Baptist Church established?

A. Silver Bluff, 1773.

———◆———

Q. The center area of which Georgia city is the largest National Historic District in the United States?

A. Savannah.

———◆———

Q. Who was the first minister to serve in the colony of Georgia?

A. Reverend Henry Herbert, an Anglican clergyman.

———◆———

Q. Who was the controversial Cabinet member appointed by President Jimmy Carter as Attorney General of the United States?

A. Griffin B. Bell.

———◆———

Q. What Georgia community was one of the few American cities not to change the English names of their streets during the Revolution?

A. Brunswick.

———◆———

Q. In which two counties were the first free county schools for all classes established in 1860?

A. Gordon and Gilmer counties.

Q. A law passed in 1832 prohibited Cherokee Indians from engaging in what activity?

A. The holding of public meetings.

———◆———

Q. What building served as the first statehouse in Atlanta?

A. The Atlanta City Hall, Fulton County Courthouse.

———◆———

Q. How many troops did Georgia provide for the Confederate cause during the four years of the War Between the States?

A. Nearly 125,000.

———◆———

Q. What was the name of the one-way shallow wooden barges used to ship cotton down-river to market towns?

A. Cottonboxes.

———◆———

Q. The oldest Baptist Church in Georgia, the Old Kiokee Baptist Church near Appling, was established in what year?

A. 1771.

———◆———

Q. In 1749 the law prohibiting what practice in the Georgia colony was repealed?

A. Slaveholding.

———◆———

Q. Where was the Battle of Bloody Marsh, in which the English scored a decisive victory over the Spanish, fought on July 7, 1742?

A. St. Simons Island.

Q. The city of Perry is named for what naval hero?

A. Commodore Oliver Hazard Perry.

Q. The Vann House, situated near Chatsworth, holds what distinction?

A. It is the only mansion in America built by an American Indian, Chief Joseph Vann.

Q. Who is known as the father of Georgia's public school system?

A. Gustavus J. Orr.

Q. What was the name of the Cherokee capital located in Gordon County?

A. New Echota.

Q. What does the ship on the back side of the state seal represent?

A. Georgia's exports.

Q. How did Georgia congressman Rufus E. Lester die in Washington, D.C., in 1906?

A. By falling through a hotel skylight.

Q. How much gunpowder was manufactured at the Confederate Powder Works in Augusta?

A. More than two million pounds of gunpowder.

Q. The Macon Confederate Museum is housed in what historic home built in 1853 by Judge Asa Holt?

A. The Old Cannonball House.

———◆———

Q. Who was the French black man who founded a school in Savannah for free black children in 1818?

A. Julien Froumontaine.

———◆———

Q. Dr. Joseph Jacobs, a young Atlanta druggist, started a new retail concept by introducing what new item to retail trade?

A. The penny.

———◆———

Q. What educational institution was established in the old State Capitol Building at Milledgeville in 1879?

A. Georgia Military College.

———◆———

Q. What were the three requirements issued by President Andrew Johnson in order for Georgia to be readmitted to the Union?

A. The emancipation of slaves, repudiation of Confederate war debts and repeal of secession ordinances.

———◆———

Q. What exposition was held in the 1880s that brought national attention to Atlanta as a manufacturing, distribution and transportation center?

A. The International Cotton Exposition.

———◆———

Q. Where was the largest sawmill in the South established in the mid-1800s?

A. Lumber City, Telfair County.

Q. In what year did the Georgia gold rush start?

A. 1828.

———◆———

Q. By what nickname was the Revolutionary War General Francis Marion, for whom Marion County was named, known?

A. "Swamp Fox."

———◆———

Q. What Marietta-born soldier served as commander in chief of the United States armed forces in Europe and as military governor of the American zone in Germany from 1947 to 1949?

A. Lucius D. Clay.

———◆———

Q. What facility at the State Sanitorium, Milledgeville, now named Central State Hospital, is the largest of its kind in the world?

A. The world's largest kitchen, capable of preparing approximately 30,000 meals a day.

———◆———

Q. What was the name of a woolen cloth produced in Georgia in the 1830s to compete with English imports?

A. Georgia Plains.

———◆———

Q. In what Georgia community was the first kindergarten in the United States established?

A. Madison.

———◆———

Q. Who presented the Capitoline statue of Romulus and Remus to the city of Rome, Georgia in 1929?

A. The Governor of Rome, Italy.

Q. How many pounds of silk were shipped from throughout Georgia to Savannah in 1764, the peak year of silk production in the colony?

A. More than 15,000 pounds.

———◆———

Q. During the Depression, what percentage of Georgia farm families were on county relief rolls?

A. Approximately 12 per cent.

———◆———

Q. Following the War Between the States, what name was given to tenant farmers who paid for the rental of the land they worked and bought their daily supplies with a percentage of the crops they produced?

A. Sharecroppers.

———◆———

Q. Who became the first Republican presidential candidate ever to win the electoral votes of Georgia?

A. Barry M. Goldwater, 1964.

———◆———

Q. In what year was the State Board of Penal Corrections created?

A. 1939.

———◆———

Q. What is the name of the locomotive housed at the Big Shanty Museum in Kennesaw that took part in the Great Locomotive Chase of War Between the States fame?

A. *The General.*

———◆———

Q. What town served as capital of Georgia from 1795 until 1804?

A. Louisville.

Q. Charles Wesley served in what capacity for James Oglethorpe?

A. His personal secretary.

◆

Q. What name was given to the 1,400-acre interracial commune established in 1942 by Clarence Jordon in Sumter County?

A. Koinonia Farms.

◆

Q. The Marietta National Cemetery contains the graves of how many Union soldiers who died during Sherman's famous "March to the Sea"?

A. 10,000 graves.

◆

Q. To whom did the state grant a monopoly in 1814 for steam navigation on all Georgia streams?

A. Samuel Howard.

◆

Q. Who was the famous 1890s evangelist whose home, Roselawn, may be seen in Cartersville?

A. Evangelist Sam P. Jones.

◆

Q. What was the name of the first steamship to cross the Atlantic in 1819, owned and operated by the Savannah Steamship Company?

A. The *Savannah*.

◆

Q. What was the actual name of the notorious pirate called "Blackbeard" who in 1716 established his headquarters on what today is named Blackbeard Island?

A. Edward Teach.

Q. What was the name of the ship on which the first colonists of Georgia arrived?

A. The *Anne*.

Q. The ambitious sculpturing project on Stone Mountain begun in 1923 was completed in what year?

A. 1969.

Q. What acting governor of Georgia (in 1777) was later killed in a duel by General Lachlan McIntosh because of rivalry for the post of Brigadier General of troops raised in Georgia?

A. Button Gwinnett.

Q. Walter F. George, born near Preston, was appointed by President Dwight D. Eisenhower as ambassador to what organization?

A. North Atlantic Treaty Organization.

Q. What legislation on education was enacted in 1916?

A. Compulsory school law.

Q. What action was taken against Georgia in 1867 for refusing to ratify the Fourteenth Amendment giving blacks full citizenship?

A. Congress placed Georgia under military rule.

Q. Where was the only Methodist Church in Georgia in 1865?

A. Epworth, in Fannin County.

Q. Richmond Academy, the first free government-supported high school, was established in which city?

A. Augusta, 1783.

———◆———

Q. What Georgian was the recipient of the 1964 Nobel Peace Prize?

A. Dr. Martin Luther King, Jr.

———◆———

Q. Lumpkin is the home of what famous inn, built in approximately 1836?

A. Bedingfield Inn.

———◆———

Q. What fort did Governor Joseph E. Brown order occupied by state troops sixteen days prior to the state's secession from the Union?

A. Fort Pulaski, near Savannah.

———◆———

Q. What organization formed in 1867 was instrumental in persuading the legislature to pass adequate educational laws?

A. The State Teachers Associatioin.

———◆———

Q. Who were the two major Indian tribes in Georgia in colonial days?

A. Creek and Cherokee.

———◆———

Q. How much money was appropriated in 1883 by the state legislature for the construction of the capitol building in Atlanta?

A. $1,000,000.

Q. Who was the notorious Reconstruction Era governor who eventually resigned and fled the state?

A. Rufus Bullock, 1868—1870.

———◆———

Q. Who originally planned the city of Brunswick?

A. General James E. Oglethorpe.

———◆———

Q. What friendly agriculture people of the Creek tribe are honored by a monument near Leesburg?

A. The Chehaw Indians.

———◆———

Q. Where was the first experimental five-mile strip of concrete highway constructed in the state in 1919?

A. North of Griffin.

———◆———

Q. Georgia State University of Atlanta evolved from what educational facility founded in 1913?

A. Georgia Tech Evening School of Commerce.

———◆———

Q. When did the first automobiles, shipped in wooden packing cases, arrive in Atlanta?

A. 1901.

———◆———

Q. What famous document did Button Gwinnett, Lyman Hall and George Walton sign?

A. The Declaration of Independence.

Q. The mother of which United States President spent her girlhood days at Roswell?

A. President Theodore Roosevelt.

Q. In 1788 Alexander Bissell of St. Simons Island was the first person to export what product to England?

A. Cotton.

Q. Which governor was known as "the one-eyed plowboy from Pigeon Roost"?

A. Allen Daniel Candler, 1898—1902.

Q. What former coastal defense fortress located on Long Island was declared a national monument in 1924?

A. Fort Pulaski.

Q. What was the name of the first brewery built in the state, used to supply ale to troops and settlers at Fort Frederica?

A. Horton's Brewery.

Q. What was the nature of the resolution passed by the legislature of South Carolina in the Fall of 1776 and presented to the lawmakers of Georgia?

A. The proposed merger of the two states.

Q. Who established and operated an academy for a short time near Eatonton as a young man and later purchased Alaska for the United States?

A. William H. Seward.

Q. Who was the first Royal Governor of Georgia?

A. John Reynolds, 1754—1757.

———◆———

Q. Red Clay was the last site for what function of the eastern band of the Cherokee Nation?

A. The last council grounds.

———◆———

Q. When was the charter establishing the colony of Georgia signed in England?

A. June 9, 1732.

———◆———

Q. In the founding of the thirteen original colonies, where did Georgia rank chronologically?

A. Thirteenth.

———◆———

Q. Who in 1717 first applied the name *Golden Isles* to the coastal islands of the state?

A. Sir Robert Montgomery.

———◆———

Q. For what sum of money did Asa Griggs Candler, Sr. become the sole owner of Coca Cola in 1891?

A. $2,300.

———◆———

Q. Who was the heroic Polish count who was mortally wounded at the siege of Savannah, October 9, 1779?

A. Casimir Pulaski.

Q. As Union forces drew near to Atlanta in June, 1864, Governor Brown made a desperate call for recruits who became known by what name?

A. *Joe Brown Malish.*

———◆———

Q. What Georgian organized the first Girl Scout troop in 1912?

A. Juliette Gordon Low.

———◆———

Q. Why did Augusta escape the wrath of General Sherman in the War Between the States?

A. It is said that he spared the city because he had loved a girl who lived there.

———◆———

Q. Georgia Southern College in Statesboro originally opened classes in 1908 under what name?

A. First District Agricultural and Mechanical High School.

———◆———

Q. The Altama Plantation, which was established in Glynn County in 1815, was purchased by which religious sect in 1898?

A. The Shakers.

———◆———

Q. Which house built in Valdosta in 1898 boasts a third-floor ballroom with the capacity of seating 300 guests?

A. The Crescent House.

———◆———

Q. What was the name of the short-lived anti-black labor movement that swept across the state in the late summer and fall of 1930?

A. The American Fascisti Association and Order of Black Shirts.

Q. What did Jimmy Carter do to help honor notable black Georgians while he was governor?

A. He appointed a committee in 1973 to nominate blacks for the portrait galleries in the State Capitol.

◆

Q. What community is considered to be the only surviving example of a complete " Federal Period" city?

A. Milledgeville.

◆

Q. What was the name of the first major anti-British organization in the Georgia colony?

A. The Liberty Boys, 1765.

◆

Q. The original state constitution in 1777 provided for what type of institutions to "be erected and supported at the general expense of the state" in each county?

A. Schools.

◆

Q. How many Union prisoners died at the Confederate POW camp at Andersonville during its fourteen month existence?

A. Over 12,900.

◆

Q. Who was the first Georgia governor elected by popular vote?

A. George Michael Troup, 1823—1827.

◆

Q. As a royal province of England, where was Georgia's first capital?

A. Savannah.

Q. At one time Augusta was the largest inland market in the world of what commodity?

A. Cotton.

Q. Spelman College in Atlanta was the first school to grant what type of certificate to a black student?

A. A nursing certificate, 1881.

Q. What event took place at the Jekyll Island Club in 1915 that made communication history?

A. The first transcontinental telephone call was made.

Q. During the Franklin Roosevelt administration, Atlanta was selected as the first city to receive government funding for what type of project?

A. Slum clearance.

Q. Which three famous Confederate personages are memorialized on the site of Stone Mountain?

A. Jefferson Davis, Robert E. Lee and Stonewall Jackson.

Q. Who was Georgia's first Chief Justice?

A. Joseph Henry Lumkin.

Q. Which engagement of Confederate and Union troops is known as the two bloodiest days of the War Between the States?

A. The Battle of Chickamauga, September 19-20, 1863.

Q. With what church did the Assembly of Georgia declare official adherence in 1758?

A. The Church of England.

---◆---

Q. By what name was the acquisition of 35 million acres of Georgia's territory for less than 1 1/2 cents per acre by unscrupulous land companies in 1795 known?

A. The Yazoo fraud.

---◆---

Q. What social program for the elderly was enacted in 1937 by the state legislature?

A. Old age insurance and related social security legislation.

---◆---

Q. A state prohibition law was passed in what year?

A. 1907, repealed in 1938.

---◆---

Q. What political party has controlled Georgia politics throughout most of the state's history?

A. The Democratic Party.

---◆---

Q. Approximately how many Union soldiers accompanied General Sherman on his "March to the Sea"?

A. Approximately 60,000.

---◆---

Q. What future president of the United States grew up in Augusta during the War Between the States?

A. Woodrow Wilson.

Q. When did General Sherman's army set fire to Atlanta?

A. November 14, 1864.

Q. In what year did high schools become a part of the state's public educational system?

A. 1912.

Q. What Confederate memorial is located in Thomson-McDuffie County?

A. A monument to Confederate women.

Q. Who founded the first Sunday school in the colony of Georgia?

A. John Wesley.

Q. Until 1908, what group of people could be leased by the state to private individuals or companies for manual labor?

A. Convicts.

Q. The convergence of the Western and Atlantic, the Macon and Western and the Georgia railroads, which eventually would become the site of present-day Atlanta, was first known by what name?

A. Terminus.

Q. For what purpose was Gammon Theological Seminary founded in Atlanta in 1883?

A. For the education of black ministers.

Q. Which of the Golden Isles is named for the Indian word for salt?

A. Tybee Island.

Q. What railroad line was completed in 1843 from Savannah to Macon?

A. The Central of Georgia.

Q. By what name was the present site of Atlanta known from 1842 to 1845?

A. Marthasville.

Q. Where was the bell cast that was located in the old market in Louisville?

A. France, 1772.

Q. Where was Jefferson Davis, president of the Confederacy, captured on May 16, 1865?

A. Approximately two miles north of Irwinville.

Q. What years was Louisville the state capital?

A. 1796—1805.

Q. What act of nature leveled all but one column of the old Slave Market in Augusta in 1878?

A. A cyclone.

Q. Who were the first Roman Catholics to be admitted into Georgia?

A. Irish Redemptionists who had pledged service for passage to the New World.

———◆———

Q. What emblem of freedom was brought to Atlanta for display in the Cotton States and International Exposition parade of 1895.

A. The Liberty Bell.

———◆———

Q. What event of January 1866 greatly helped foster better educational opportunities for blacks?

A. The formation of a black educational association.

———◆———

Q. In 1916 which department of the state government served as a highway board?

A. The state prison board.

———◆———

Q. What years did Augusta serve as the state's capital?

A. 1783—1795.

———◆———

Q. In 1906 the legislature enacted a law prohibiting the employment of what segment of the population?

A. Children under ten years of age.

———◆———

Q. What was the name of the Jewish welfare service formed in Atlanta during the War Between the States?

A. The Hebrew Benevolent Society.

Q. What political office in Georgia was held by Jimmy Carter previous to being elected President of the United States?

A. Governor, 1971—1975.

---◆---

Q. What was the annual salary approved in 1743 by the common council of Savannah for a teacher to serve in the city's free school?

A. 20 pounds sterling.

---◆---

Q. Which institution on January 27, 1785 became the first state university to be chartered in America?

A. The University of Georgia.

---◆---

Q. In 1825 Governor George M. Troup declared that a state of war would exist between Georgia and the United States if the federal government did not carry out what process?

A. The removal of Creek Indians from Georgia.

---◆---

Q. In 1836 which college became the first in the world chartered to grant degrees exclusively to women?

A. The Georgia Female College, Macon (renamed Wesleyan College).

---◆---

Q. What is the date of Georgia Day?

A. February 12.

---◆---

Q. In 1874 Georgia led the nation in establishing what state department?

A. The Georgia Department of Agriculture.

Q. Who was governor of Georgia during the War Between the States, and the only Georgia governor to serve four terms?

A. Joe E. Brown.

Q. Where was the first printed cotton cloth produced in the state?

A. John Shly's textile mill near Augusta, around 1834.

Q. In December 1829 the legislature made what activity with blacks illegal?

A. The education of blacks, slave or free.

Q. In what year was Georgia readmitted into the Union?

A. 1870.

Q. Who is said to have greeted every ship that entered the Port of Savannah from 1887 to 1931 and is honored by a statue of a waving girl in Riverfront Plaza?

A. Florence Martus.

Q. What United States president practiced law in Atlanta as a young man from 1882 to 1883?

A. Woodrow Wilson.

Q. What early American explorer, soldier and political leader born in Savannah was nicknamed "The Pathfinder" because of his explorations between the Rocky Mountains and the Pacific Ocean?

A. John Charles Frémont.

Q. What year was Atlanta's first full-time police force established?

A. 1873.

Q. What was the dollar amount of the property damage that General Sherman estimated his army cost Georgia?

A. One million dollars.

Q. Who was the young lady from Knoxville in Crawford County who designed the famous "Lone Star" flag of Texas?

A. Joanna E. Troutman.

Q. What man served 34 years in the United States Senate, never losing an election and having the Law School at Mercer University named in his honor?

A. Walter F. George.

Q. A hurriedly enacted law following the discovery of gold in northern Georgia in 1828 denied what basic civil rights to Cherokee Indians?

A. The right to sue or testify against a white man.

Q. Who was the noted Methodist churchman who held the first Methodist Conference near Elberton in 1788?

A. Bishop Francis Asbury.

Q. In 1754 Georgia received what status with England?

A. Royal province.

Q. The state constitution of 1877 institutionalized what practice in education?

A. The segregated school system.

———◆———

Q. The Old Greene County "Gaol" Rock jail built in 1807 in Greensboro imitates what architectural style?

A. Bastilles of the 19th century.

———◆———

Q. When was an independent highway board created within the state government?

A. 1919.

———◆———

Q. What was the occupation of R. M. Harding, for whom Lake Harding on the Chattahoochee River was named in 1926?

A. General manager of the Columbus Electric and Power Company.

———◆———

Q. What heroic young colonel from Georgia died at Fort Goliad in 1836 during the War of Texas Independence?

A. Colonel James W. Fannin.

———◆———

Q. Based on Governor James Wright's estimated figures, what was the population of Georgia in 1766?

A. 10,000 whites and 7,800 blacks.

———◆———

Q. On what date was Atlanta first illuminated by a new gas lighting system?

A. December 25, 1855.

Q. What was the occupation of William Berry Hartsfield, for whom the Hartsfield International Airport in Atlanta was named in 1970?

A. Mayor of Atlanta, 1937—1960.

◆

Q. Small rural elementary schools operated without state or county control in the early 19th century were known by what name?

A. Old Field Schools.

◆

Q. In what year did the Creek Indians leave Georgia and move west of the Mississippi River?

A. 1826.

◆

Q. What black preacher, with the aid of Reverend Abraham Marshall, organized the First African Baptist Church in Savannah in 1788?

A. Jesse Peters.

◆

Q. The first Presbyterian colonists who settled at Darien in 1735 were of what ethnic background?

A. Scottish Highlanders.

◆

Q. Who organized the first state fair at Stone Mountain in 1846?

A. The South Central Agricultural Society.

◆

Q. What was the seemingly excessive construction price of an Augusta Federal style home built in 1818 that led to its being named *Ware's Folly*?

A. $40,000.

Q. What were the Cherokee Indians offered in 1835 to give up their Georgia holdings?

A. $5,000,000 and relocation in the West.

Q. Who was the governor from 1827-1829 who also served as secretary of state under President Van Buren?

A. John Forsyth.

Q. James Hamilton, who established the Hamilton Plantation on St. Simons Island in 1804, was a native of what country?

A. Scotland.

Q. Who was the first Presbyterian evangelist to enter Georgia?

A. Reverend John Newton, in 1785.

Q. What collective group of boards was originally vested with the supervision of all public educational activities within the state?

A. Senatus Academicus.

Q. Who in 1757 built Fort Ebenezer, in what became Effingham County, to protect settlers from Indian attacks?

A. John Gerar William DeBrahm.

Q. What community, at one time located across the Ocmulgee River from Hawkinsville, came within one vote of becoming the state capital in 1804?

A. Hartford, in Pulaski County.

ARTS & LITERATURE

CHAPTER FOUR

Q. Who is the internationally recognized Georgia writer known for such works as her St. Simons Trilogy comprised of *Lighthouse, New Moon Rising* and *Beloved Invader*?

A. Eugenia Price.

Q. Which cartoon strip series was based on characters who lived in the Okefenokee Swamp?

A. Pogo.

Q. What is the Southeast's largest professional non-profit theater group?

A. The Alliance Theatre, Atlanta.

Q. Rabun County high-school teacher Eliot Wigginton is editor of what series of best-selling books?

A. *Foxfire.*

Q. Which Georgia-born gospel music composer wrote such classics as *Where No One Stands Alone, Till the Storm Passes By, Then I Met the Master* and *How Long Has It Been*?

A. Mosie Lister.

Q. St. Simons Island resident Joyce Blackburn is known for what series of children's books?

A. The *Suki* series.

———◆———

Q. Where was the United Sacred Harp Musical Association founded and headquartered in 1904?

A. Atlanta.

———◆———

Q. What pioneer journal in the field of medicine was established in Augusta in 1845?

A. *Southern Medical and Surgical Journal.*

———◆———

Q. What book by Georgia-born Rosey Grier was published in 1973?

A. *Rosey Grier Needlepoint Book for Men.*

———◆———

Q. Who was the renowned painter of miniatures who died in Savannah in 1807?

A. Edward Greene Malbone.

———◆———

Q. In 1937 *Gone With the Wind* brought its author what coveted award?

A. The Pulitzer Prize.

———◆———

Q. What is said to "Cover Dixie Like the Dew"?

A. The *Atlanta Journal.*

Q. Who was the author of *Gone With the Wind*?

A. Margaret Mitchell.

Q. Who was the internationally famous blind pianist and composer born a slave in 1849 on the Bethune plantation near Columbus?

A. Thomas Green Bethune, "Blind Tom."

Q. Joel Chandler Harris spins tales of Georgia in which popular traditional black stories?

A. Uncle Remus stories.

Q. What early radio program was broadcast on WSB in Atlanta to promote interest in the arts within the public schools?

A. *Atlanta Journal School of the Arts*.

Q. Where is the Carter Library located?

A. Southwestern College, Americus.

Q. Born in White Oak, what author is best known for the sensationalism of his novels about rural southern life?

A. Erskine Caldwell.

Q. What was the name of Georgia's first newspaper, established in Savannah in 1763?

A. *Georgia Gazette*.

Q. The seventh book by Lewis Grizzard, a native of Moreland, Coweta County, is known by what title?

A. *Shoot Low Boys, They're Ridin' Shetland Ponies.*

———◆———

Q. Which island hosts the annual Golden Isles Art Festival in October?

A. St. Simons Island.

———◆———

Q. Who composed the *Georgia Blues* in the early 1920s?

A. Billy Higgins and W. Benton Overstreet.

———◆———

Q. What opera was presented in Atlanta at The Metropolitan Opera Company's first performance on May 2, 1910?

A. *Lohengrin.*

———◆———

Q. Troup County has honored what well-known artist by naming an art center after him?

A. Lamar Dodd.

———◆———

Q. Which composer and lyricist wrote "Georgia On My Mind"?

A. Hoagy Carmichael and Stuart Gorrell.

———◆———

Q. What plantation served as the inspiration for "Twelve Oaks" in *Gone With the Wind*?

A. Lovejoy Plantation, 20 miles south of Atlanta.

Q. Who was known as "one of the world's greatest opera singers of the nineties" and kept a suite at the famous Aragon of Atlanta?

A. The "divine" Adelina Patti.

———◆———

Q. How many newspapers were there in the state by 1850?

A. 51.

———◆———

Q. In 1894, Atlanta published a new type of newspaper, a scandal sheet, under what name?

A. *The Looking Glass*.

———◆———

Q. Who was the most noted colonial Georgian potter?

A. Andrew Duché.

———◆———

Q. What Americus-born composer/guitarist wrote *Black Jazz*, *White Jazz* and *Casa Loma Stomp*?

A. Harold Eugene (Gene) Gifford.

———◆———

Q. Which one-time star reporter for the *Atlanta Constitution* wrote *Cora Potts* in 1929 and *Death in the Deep South* in 1936?

A. Ward Greene.

———◆———

Q. Who was the youthful local poet who named the community of Halcyondale, located south of Sylvania in Screven County?

A. Cuyler Young.

Q. Who organized a Georgia chapter of the American Guild of Organists in 1914?

A. Edwin Arthur Kraft.

Q. Who wrote *Some Go Up* and *Old Lady's Shoes*, both of which are set in the author's native Atlanta?

A. Samuel Tupper, Jr.

Q. Edison Marshall became nationally famous for what type of writing?

A. Adventure stories.

Q. In 1927 Marie Conway Oemler wrote which popular romance novel?

A. *Slippy McGee*.

Q. Carl Brandt, who served as director of Savannah's Telfair Academy, was best known as what type of painter?

A. Muralist.

Q. Which noted New England artist and inventor spent time painting portraits in Darien?

A. Samuel F. B. Morse.

Q. For what work is poet Robert Loveman best remembered?

A. *Rain Song*.

Q. What cartoonist created the character Mark Trail and had his comic strip collection on display at Gainesville's Green Street Station?

A. Ed Dodd.

———◆———

Q. What is the name of the oldest continuously published newspaper in the state, dating back to 1785?

A. The *Augusta Chronicle*.

———◆———

Q. Where is the home of the Columbus Symphony?

A. Three Arts Theater.

———◆———

Q. Who founded the *Columbus Enquirer* in 1828 and went on to become the president of the Republic of Texas?

A. Mirabeau Buonaparte Lamar.

———◆———

Q. What Albany native rhythm and blues singer/musician is credited with ten Grammy Awards, numerous TV appearances and several gold records and is a member of the Songwriters Hall of Fame?

A. Ray Charles.

———◆———

Q. What was the approximate building cost of Atlanta's High Museum of Art?

A. Twenty million dollars.

Q. Where did poet Sidney Lanier compose his famous "Marshes of Glynn"?

A. Lanier Oak near Brunswick.

◆

Q. The Atlanta Children's Theatre is part of what theatrical company?

A. The Alliance Theatre.

◆

Q. Which coastal area painter has become well known for paintings of the coastal cities, seascapes and ships?

A. Selma Jernigan.

◆

Q. What Atlanta artist is known in the southeast as a portrait painter and watercolorist and has done several book illustrations including those for Celestine Sibley's classic *Christmas In Georgia*?

A. Scarlett Blanton Rickenbacker.

◆

Q. What is the name of journalist Joel Chandler Harris' Atlanta home?

A. Wren's Nest.

◆

Q. During the early days of the "Met," what renowned opera singer made his first southern appearance as "Radames" in *Aida* and as "Canio" in *I Pagliacci*?

A. Enrico Caruso.

◆

Q. What was the state's first black newspaper, established in Augusta in 1865?

A. *The Colored American.*

Q. What Cuthbert-born jazz great introduced the concept of "big band" divided into brass, reed and rhythm sections?

A. Fletcher Henderson.

———◆———

Q. How many copies of *Gone With the Wind* were sold in the first six months after publication?

A. Over one million.

———◆———

Q. One of the most valuable sources of insight into pioneer life between 1737 and 1741 may be found in the journals of which early Georgian?

A. William Stephens.

———◆———

Q. Which Georgia newspaper declared in bold headlines on April 15, 1861, "War! War!! War!!! 75,000 Barbarians Coming Down on the South!"?

A. The *Macon Telegraph*.

———◆———

Q. In the pre-Revolutionary period, by what name were traveling itinerant painters known?

A. Rider artists.

———◆———

Q. Where was the birthplace of black musician Thomas Andrew Dorsey, composer/arranger of over 800 songs and internationally known for his gospel composition *There'll Be Peace in the Valley*?

A. Villa Rica.

———◆———

Q. What was the title of Rosalynn Carter's bestselling 1984—1985 book?

A. *First Lady from Plains*.

Q. What is the name of the Dillard community center for the arts, established in 1934?

A. Hambidge Center.

Q. Where did the Uncle Remus stories first appear in print?

A. The *Atlanta Constitution*.

Q. Who became the conductor of the Atlanta Philharmonic Orchestra in 1933?

A. Georg Linder.

Q. The black Big Bethel Choir of Atlanta was known for what musical folk play?

A. *Heaven Bound*.

Q. Which Savannah-born sculptor was internationally known for his bronze animal works?

A. Edward Kemeys.

Q. The adjustment of a young artist to the commercial community around him is the subject in which 1938 novel by Harry Lee?

A. *The Fox in the Cloak*.

Q. Which well-known black writer authored *Fire and Flint*?

A. Walter White.

Q. In 1955 Savannah-born Flannery O'Connor wrote a collection of short stories by what title?

A. *A Good Man Is Hard to Find.*

Q. What is the title of the book by Caroline C. Lovell concerning the history and development of Georgia's coastal islands?

A. *The Golden Isles of Georgia.*

Q. Where is the Roddenberg Memorial Library?

A. Cairo.

Q. In *Gone With the Wind*, Margaret Mitchell modeled Tara after what Atlanta antebellum home?

A. Fitzgerald House.

Q. What is the official state song, selected on April 24, 1979?

A. *Georgia On My Mind.*

Q. What Atlanta theater presents the Best of Broadway plays?

A. The Fox.

Q. Atlanta's High Museum of Art features 13th—18th century Italian paintings and Northern Italian sculpture from what collection?

A. The Samuel H. Kress Collection.

Q. What famous fiction writer was born in Alma?

A. Harry Crews.

◆

Q. Where is the home of the internationally-acclaimed Atlanta Symphony Orchestra?

A. Robert W. Woodruff Arts Center.

◆

Q. Who wrote *Road to Tara*, the life of Margaret Mitchell?

A. Anne Edwards.

◆

Q. What is the rarest antique on display in the Governor's Mansion?

A. A 19th-century French porcelain vase with a portrait medallion of Benjamin Franklin.

◆

Q. How many theatrical groups are based in Atlanta?

A. More than twenty.

◆

Q. What was Sidney Lanier's philosophical prose work which set about to prove an inseparable relationship between the laws of verse and music?

A. *The Science of English Verse*, 1880.

◆

Q. Which work of Caroline Miller won the 1934 Pulitzer Prize?

A. *Lamb In His Bosom*.

Q. What Atlanta resident is a journalist for the *Atlanta Journal* and the *Atlanta Constitution* and his works also appear regularly in over 200 newspapers nationwide?

A. Lewis Grizzard.

Q. What turn-of-the-century work by Robert Cole and William Johnson became the first successful black musical comedy written for black performers?

A. *A Trip to Coontown*.

Q. What Atlanta-born jazz composer has said "We are the interpreters of Nature's Music. We find that everything on the earth contributes to its harmony"?

A. (Norris Jones) Sirone.

Q. Which non-Georgian wrote *I Am a Fugitive from a Georgia Chain Gang*?

A. Robert W. Burns.

Q. What Atlanta organization was formed in 1909 to inaugurate the opening of the municipal auditorium and an annual music festival?

A. Atlanta Music Festival Association.

Q. Who was the noted poet, priest and long-time Augusta resident who penned such Southern Confederacy tributes as *The Conquered Banner* and *Sword of Lee*?

A. Father Ryan.

Q. Which black singer born in Tennille in 1928 won the 1947 National Competition for Soloists Award from the Boston Pops Orchestra?

A. McHenry Rutherford Boatwright.

Q. Which black opera singer born in Atlanta in 1925 has extensively toured Europe?

A. Mattiwila.

———◆———

Q. What book, edited by Jane Bonner Peacock, has given us a collection of letters written by Margaret Mitchell from 1919 to 1921?

A. *Margaret Mitchell: A Dynamo Going to Waste.*

———◆———

Q. The fabrication of a "Tar Baby" in the Uncle Remus tales is a ploy by Br'er Fox to catch which character?

A. Br'er Rabbit.

———◆———

Q. What is Georgia's oldest continuing theatrical group?

A. The Academy, formed in 1956 in Atlanta.

———◆———

Q. James Dickey composed what poem reflecting his experiences as a combat pilot?

A. *The Firebombing.*

———◆———

Q. Who was editor of the *Columbus Enquirer-Sun* in 1926 and managing editor of the *Atlanta Constitution* when both of these papers received a Pulitzer prize?

A. Julian La Rose Harris, son of Joel Chandler Harris.

———◆———

Q. Who was the noted sports writer of the 20s and 30s with the *Atlanta Journal*?

A. Grantland Rice.

Q. Stained-glass masterpieces by what two artists highlight the Faith Chapel on Jekyll Island?

A. Louis Comfort Tiffany and D. Maitland Armstrong.

---◆---

Q. The best-selling novel ever written, *Gone With the Wind*, has been translated into how many languages?

A. 36.

---◆---

Q. Lowell Mason, who composed such 19th-century hymns as *Nearer My God to Thee* and *My Faith Looks Up to Thee*, began his musical career in which Georgia city?

A. Savannah.

---◆---

Q. What Sidney Lanier poem contrasts the abundance of southern agriculture to what he thought to be the false, sterile values of northern commerce?

A. *Corn*.

---◆---

Q. What architect designed the High Museum of Art?

A. Richard Meier.

---◆---

Q. Who founded the Atlanta *Constitution* in 1868?

A. Colonel Carey W. Styles.

---◆---

Q. What book, written by Lucius D. Clay, is based on his experiences in military government?

A. *Decision in Germany*, 1950.

Q. What 1932 novel by Erskine Caldwell focuses on the poverty, ignorance and disease of the sharecropper class?

A. *Tobacco Road.*

———◆———

Q. What 50-foot-high, 400-foot circumference painting-in-the-round depicts the 1864 Civil War Battle of Atlanta?

A. Cyclorama.

———◆———

Q. What Atlanta-born pianist and composer received an award from BMI for over 1,000,000 broadcast performances of his composition, *Canadian Sunset*?

A. Eddie Heywood, Jr.

———◆———

Q. By legislative action in 1985, what person was named Georgia's "most famous citizen"?

A. Margaret Mitchell.

———◆———

Q. Which Georgian author penned the two sharply ironic novels, *The Hard-boiled Virgin* in 1926 and *Dead Lovers are Faithful Lovers* in 1928?

A. Frances Newman.

———◆———

Q. What are the character subjects in the tales of Elmer Ransom?

A. Animals.

———◆———

Q. Where is the 1918 birthplace of concert singer Carol Lovette Hawkins Brice?

A. Sedalia.

Q. *Georgia Place-Names* was published in 1975 by which Macon resident?

A. Kenneth K. Krakow.

———◆———

Q. Who was the New York native educator and clergyman who wrote the *Gazateer of the State of Georgia* in the 1820s and 30s?

A. Adiel Sherwood.

———◆———

Q. Who is the renowned conductor of the Atlanta Symphony?

A. Robert Shaw.

———◆———

Q. Who was the most popular Georgian poet of the 1890s?

A. Frank L. Stanton.

———◆———

Q. Who was the well-known 19th-century author who wrote the juvenile books *Young Marooners* in 1852 and *Marooner's' Island* in 1862?

A. F.R. Goulding.

———◆———

Q. Which Georgia city is the setting for Willie Snow Ethridge's memoirs, *As I Live and Breathe*?

A. Macon.

———◆———

Q. The rural development of a cappella singing by reading shaped-note music led to the participants being called by what name?

A. Fasola singers.

Q. What Atlanta-born poet, novelist, film-maker, and critic was known for such poems as *The Strength of the Fields*, 1979; *Scion*, 1980; and *Deliverance: A Screenplay*, 1981?

A. James Dickey.

Q. One thousand copies of what type book were presented to James Edward Oglethorpe by James Leake in January, 1732, to be used in the colony?

A. Spelling books.

Q. Where can you visit Georgia's first privately endowed public library?

A. Washington.

Q. What song was written by Stephen Foster immortalizing the Suwannee River?

A. *Old Folks at Home* (*Way Down Upon the Swanee River*).

Q. Who authored a 1982 collection of black folk tales from rural Georgia entitled *Hush, Child Can't You Hear the Music?*

A. Rose Thompson.

Q. Dalton's Creative Arts Guild for performing and visual arts is housed in what type of building?

A. The old firehouse.

Q. Who painted the murals at the U.S. Federal Building and Post Office in Macon, depicting the history of the area?

A. George Beattie.

Q. What newspaper woman penned the 1930 novel *Secret Fathers*?

A. Mildred Seydell.

———◆———

Q. What folk opera did Hall Johnson, a choir director from Athens, compose?

A. *Run, Little Chillun.*

———◆———

Q. Who wrote *History of Savannah and South Georgia* in 1913?

A. William Harden.

———◆———

Q. Where is the Springer Opera House located?

A. Columbus.

———◆———

Q. Who received national acclaim for *The Tragedy of Lynching*, a work dealing with interracial relations?

A. Arthur Raper.

———◆———

Q. In what year was the Savannah Music Club formed?

A. 1897.

———◆———

Q. Who was awarded the 1896 *Chicago Record* prize for his work *Sons and Fathers*?

A. Harry Stillwell Edwards.

Q. What Georgia-born writer produced *Member of the Wedding*?

A. Carson McCullers.

Q. The Douglas County community of Bill Arp was named for the pen-name of which southern humorist/newspaper editor?

A. Charles Henry Smith.

Q. What Atlanta-born composer was the only non-Ellington alumnus to perform for the Duke Ellington Society and arrange the music for Ellington's 74th birthday party?

A. Columbus Calvin (Duke) Pearson, Jr.

Q. Georgian writer, Berry Fleming, is best known for what 1935 novel with a southern setting?

A. *Siesta.*

Q. Who edited the Atlanta *Constitution* from 1879 until his death and was known as the voice of the "New South"?

A. Henry Woodfin Grady (1850—1889).

Q. Nineteenth-century painter William Posey Silva is best known for what subject matter?

A. Landscapes.

Q. Which play by Lula Vollmer served as a vivid dramatization of southern mountaineer life?

A. *Sun Up*, 1924.

Q. Where is the Uncle Remus Museum and Statue honoring the works of Joel Chandler Harris?

A. Eatonton.

———◆———

Q. Which Georgia biographer is known for her works on Martha Berry, James Oglethorpe, Theodore Roosevelt, John Adams and George Wythe?

A. Joyce Blackburn.

———◆———

Q. What was the first book by Corra Harris which brought her to national attention in 1910?

A. *A Circuit Rider's Wife.*

———◆———

Q. What serial written and published by Baldwin Longstreet in the *Augusta Sentinel* humorously depicted the vigorous lifestyles of Georgians in the 1830s?

A. *Georgia Scenes.*

———◆———

Q. Who authored the well-known state historical book, *A Short History of Georgia*?

A. Merton Coulter.

———◆———

Q. Where did Rembrandt and Raphael Peale establish a shop in 1804 to produce portraits, silhouettes and miniatures?

A. Savannah.

———◆———

Q. Who wrote the 1938 novel *Mingled Yarn*, dealing with the problems of a young mill town couple?

A. Willie Snow Ethridge.

Q. Who was the first American woman to own and edit a newspaper?

A. Sarah Porter Hillhouse, *The Washington Gazette*.

◆

Q. The *Story of France*, 1898, and *Napoleon*, 1903, are works of what turn-of-the-century Georgian writer?

A. Thomas E. Watson.

◆

Q. What was the name of the hymnal compiled by John Wesley in Savannah which became the first Methodist hymnal ever published?

A. *A Collection of Psalms and Hymns*.

◆

Q. What book by Atlanta journalist Celestine Sibley depicts southern life?

A. *For All Seasons*.

◆

Q. What type of programming was first featured on radio station WSB in Atlanta?

A. Regular nightly programs.

◆

Q. Thomas and Lucy Carnegie built their magnificent *Dungeness* on what island?

A. Cumberland Island.

◆

Q. What Confederate army general was elected to the Georgia Senate, served as governor and published the book *Reminiscences of the Civil War*?

A. John Brown Gordon (1832-1904).

Q. The famous "unfinished portrait" of Franklin D. Roosevelt hangs in what museum?

A. Franklin D. Roosevelt Museum at Warm Springs.

―――◆―――

Q. Where in Albany can a variety of comedies, musicals, dramas and children's theater productions be viewed?

A. Little Theatre.

―――◆―――

Q. The Macon City Auditorium is home for what large instrument?

A. Pipe organ.

―――◆―――

Q. Which Georgia newspaper won a 1937 Pulitzer prize?

A. The *Atlanta Journal*.

―――◆―――

Q. What 1906 book published by Augustus Longstreet Hull deals with the settlement and development of Athens?

A. *Annals of Athens, Georgia, 1801—1901*.

―――◆―――

Q. Who was the poet, noted for his tortuous idioms and overornamentation, who published *The Lost Pleiad and Other Poems* in 1842?

A. Thomas Holley Chivers.

―――◆―――

Q. Who won the 1930 annual award of the Poetry Society of America for his work *Strange Splendor*?

A. Ernest Hartsock.

Q. What opera company was first heard in Augusta in 1854?

A. The New Orleans Opera Company.

———◆———

Q. What 1935 work by Walter Mills analyzes the propaganda which aroused America to participate in World War I?

A. *Road to War.*

———◆———

Q. In 1900 what world renowned pianist, who later became Poland's president, gave a recital at the Grand Theater?

A. Ignace Jan Paderewski.

———◆———

Q. Though often a writer of novels with a foreign setting, Isa Glenn wrote what book in 1930 set in Georgia?

A. *A Short History of Julia.*

———◆———

Q. Name the three best-known animal characters in the famous Uncle Remus stories?

A. Br'er Rabbit, Br'er Fox and Br'er Bear.

———◆———

Q. The classic Renaissance style capitol building in Atlanta was designed by what architectural firm?

A. Edbrooke and Burnham of Chicago.

———◆———

Q. A widely publicized 19th-century murder case led to what ballad?

A. *The Death of Mary Fagan.*

SPORTS & LEISURE

C H A P T E R   F I V E

Q. What team were the Atlanta Braves playing when Hank Aaron broke Babe Ruth's home run record?

A. Los Angeles Dodgers, April 8, 1974.

Q. What city hosts the Georgia State Fair each October?

A. Macon, since 1851.

Q. What was the name of the nine-hole golf course built for the millionaire members of the Jekyll Island Club?

A. Oceanside Nine.

Q. What Georgia Bulldog received the Heisman Trophy in 1982?

A. Herschel Walker.

Q. What Bainbridge-born top boxing contender lost only 15 of 127 professional fights?

A. William Lawrence (Young) Stribling, II.

Q. What Georgian-born baseball player was the first black man to play major league ball?

A. Jackie Robinson.

———◆———

Q. Which family owned Jekyll Island prior to the millionaires?

A. The du Bignon family.

———◆———

Q. What fullback for the Cleveland Browns was born on St. Simons Island and led the National Football League in rushing for eight of his nine years of play?

A. Jim Brown.

———◆———

Q. In what year was the National Baseball League established, of which the Braves are charter members?

A. 1876.

———◆———

Q. What Walthourville native became the only cyclist to hold the national and world titles simultaneously and was known as the "Dixie Worldwind"?

A. Bobby Walthour, Sr.

———◆———

Q. Fitzgerald, which originated as a Union soldiers' colony, is now home for what museum?

A. The Blue Gray Museum.

———◆———

Q. The Lookout Mountain Flight Park is the site of what exciting sport?

A. Hang gliding.

Q. Who purchased the Atlanta Braves in 1976?

A. R. E. "Ted" Turner.

———◆———

Q. Who is known as the "Sports Doc," the founder and director of the Hughston Sports Medicine Hospital and Campus in Columbus?

A. Jack Hughston.

———◆———

Q. Who was the University of Georgia athlete who won the hurdles championship at the 1936 Olympics?

A. Forrest "Spec" Towns.

———◆———

Q. What part of the Flint River is said to have destroyed more canoes than any other single rapid in the southeast?

A. Yellow Jacket Shoals.

———◆———

Q. What is the name of the collection of authenic log cabins on display at Fort Gaines?

A. Frontier Village.

———◆———

Q. Georgia defeated Texas 10-9 in what 1984 bowl game?
A. Cotton Bowl.

———◆———

Q. What governor signed into law the bill to create the Georgia Sports Hall of Fame?

A. Governor George Busbee, 1978.

Q. On May 7, 1985, what favorite New York Knicks player became assistant coach with the Altanta Hawks?

A. Willis Reed.

———◆———

Q. Sam Jones (Sambo) Elliott, McDonough native, was elected to what Hall of Fame in 1957?

A. The National Softball Hall of Fame.

———◆———

Q. The Falcon Training Complex, year-round home of the Falcons, is located in what community?

A. Suwannee.

———◆———

Q. Which Georgian won the 1938 black national golf championship?

A. Howard Wheeler.

———◆———

Q. Which lake has been called the "Houseboat Capital of the World"?

A. Lanier Lake.

———◆———

Q. Who was the Georgian who won the national clay courts tennis championship in 1930, 1934 and 1935?

A. Bryan "Bitsy" Grant.

———◆———

Q. What University of Georgia football player received the South's first Heisman Trophy in 1942?

A. Frank Sinkwich.

Q. What Atlanta-born golfer was the women pro tour's leading money winner from 1953 to 1960?

A. Louise Suggs.

——◆——

Q. What are the school colors of Georgia State University, Atlanta?

A. Royal Blue and Sky Blue.

——◆——

Q. At what location in Savannah can you see a classic 1920 gold-and-silver-plated Pierce Arrow?

A. Evans Antique Car Museums.

——◆——

Q. What Atlanta Brave pitched a no-hitter over San Diego, August 5, 1973?

A. Phil Niekro.

——◆——

Q. Who was "Best Athlete" at Lanier High 1943—1945 and earned 11 letters at Georgia Tech before beginning an outstanding coaching career?

A. Jim Nolan.

——◆——

Q. In 1927, who led the New York Giants to the World championship after being All-Southern fullback for Georgia Tech three straight years (1923—1925)?

A. Doug Wycoff.

——◆——

Q. Beginning the first Saturday in November and ending the last Saturday in March, Thomson participants dress in scarlet and black for what sporting event?

A. The Belle Meade Fox Hunt.

Q. Born in Atlanta in 1938, Mack Jones played outfield during a ten-year period for the Milwaukee Braves, Atlanta Braves, Cincinnati Reds and Montreal Expos and was known by what nickname?

A. Mack "The Knife" Jones.

Q. What was the great national sport of the Cherokee of Georgia?

A. Stick ball or ball-play, a form of Lacrosse.

Q. Who is the Rome-born Atlanta Hawk whose father was head basketball coach at the Georgia School for the Deaf?

A. Mike Glenn.

Q. Augusta is the home of what internationally-famous golfing event?

A. The Master's Golf Tournament.

Q. Claxton and Wigham are noted for what type of yearly roundups?

A. Rattlesnake.

Q. Before moving to Atlanta, the Braves were associated with what two cities?

A. Boston and Milwaukee.

Q. What Carrollton native was known as the "Adolph Rupp of Georgia high school basketball"?

A. Eric P. Staples.

Q. Beau Jack, shoeshine boy at Augusta National, later held what famous world championship title?

A. World lightweight boxing champion.

◆

Q. What Georgia Tech coach and National Hall of Famer was the first to coach six major bowl winners in consecutive years and coached the All-Stars in the Miami North-South Shrine game (1950—1957)?

A. Robert Lee (Bobby) Dodd.

◆

Q. The Washington-Wilkes Historical Museum in Washington is noted for what type of Civil War memorabilia collection?

A. Confederate gun collection.

◆

Q. On July 24, 1984, the Hawks signed what top 1984 draft choice?

A. Kevin Willis.

◆

Q. In what city is the Chieftains Museum located?
A. Rome.

◆

Q. Known as a great relief pitcher, what Buckhead-born player won fame in the 1940s with the Brooklyn Dodgers?

A. Hugh Casey.

◆

Q. Len Hauss of Washington Redskin fame is from what community?

A. Jesup.

Q. Where was the birthplace of professional ball player Jackie Robinson?

A. Cairo.

Q. Where would you find one of the finest ships-in-a-bottle collections in the world?

A. Ships of the Sea, a Maritime Museum in Savannah.

Q. What former University of Georgia football coach was immortalized and given the title "Great White Football Father"?

A. Pop Warner.

Q. Who is the Falcon's all-time leading rusher?

A. William Andrews.

Q. Who was the Macon-born favorite L.A. Dodger, known as "Mr. Clutch."

A. Ronald Ray Fairly.

Q. What Toccoa High athlete gained fame by winning the Gold Medal in the 1956 Olympics, making him "The World's Strongest Man"?

A. Paul Anderson.

Q. What Georgia Tech coach was the first to put his team in all the major bowls, Rose (1928), Orange (1939 & 1944), Cotton (1942) and Sugar (1943)?

A. W. A. Alexander.

Q. What professional baseball player was nicknamed the "Georgia Peach"?

A. Ty Cobb (Tyrus Raymond Cobb).

———◆———

Q. Where is the world's largest man-made sand beach?

A. Callaway Gardens.

———◆———

Q. Which annual crafts fair has its home in Chatsworth?

A. Ft. Mountain Village Crafts Fair.

———◆———

Q. What All-American and All-Southeastern Conference guard at Georgia Tech, 1951, later became affiliated with the New York Giants?

A. Ray Beck.

———◆———

Q. What Atlanta lady golfer realized her goal of winning the USGA's national women's amateur golf championship in 1951?

A. Dorothy (Dot) Kirby.

———◆———

Q. What collegiate football bowl takes place in Atlanta?

A. Peach Bowl.

———◆———

Q. Who became the first athlete to win an Olympic Gold Medal while representing a southern school?

A. Edward B. Hamm, Georgia Tech Track (1926-30).

Q. What Fall festival is held in Camilla?

A. The Corn Festival.

———◆———

Q. What Buchanan farmer took the 1954 Crackers to a win of the Southern Association pennant, all-star games, playoffs and Dixie Series?

A. John Whitlow Wyatt.

———◆———

Q. Who was Georgia's first selection for the National Football Hall of Fame?

A. Robert (Bob) McWhorter.

———◆———

Q. What is probably the most famous annual Georgia event?

A. The Master's Golf Tournament, the second week in April.

———◆———

Q. Columbus Drive Field, Cobb County, is the home of what aristocratic sport?

A. Polo.

———◆———

Q. What Atlanta Hawk holds the high point record for a single season's performance?

A. Dominique Wilkins, 2,217 points (1984—1985).

———◆———

Q. What Atlanta race car driver became NASCAR's first "king of the oval tracks" by winning 40 races in fewer than 250 starts through 1956?

A. Tim Flock.

Q. What football pro from Athens High School threw more passes for more yards, more completions and more touchdowns than anyone in NFL history?

A. Francis Asbury (Fran) Tarkenton.

◆

Q. What Tech High football star played for the New York Giants and became the only back to win back-to-back NFL rushing titles his first two pro seasons (1943—1944)?

A. Billy Paschal.

◆

Q. What World Wrestling Federation champ nicknamed "Mr. Wonderful" now resides in Atlanta?

A. Paul Orndorff.

◆

Q. Wyomia Tyus, track star who began training at Fairmount High in Griffin, brought home the gold, winning the 100-yard dash in what Olympics?

A. 1964 Olympics, Tokyo.

◆

Q. The Atlanta International Raceway hosts what two Grand National stock car races?

A. The Atlanta Journal 500 and the Coca Cola 500.

◆

Q. Pine Mountain, between Warm Springs and Callaway, offers a swimming pool in what unforgettable shape?

A. The Liberty Bell.

◆

Q. Besides Braves Baseball and Falcon Football, what other two sporting events are held annually at the Atlanta-Fulton County Stadium?

A. Peach Bowl and Motocross race.

Q. Who coached Gainesville to a state basketball title in 1949?

A. Drane Watson.

Q. What community is the home of the nationwide Chick-fil-A chain?

A. Hapeville.

Q. What Georgia-born sportsman of the early 30s known as the "Emperor of Golf," won the American Amateur, the American Open, the British Amateur and the British Open, all within one year?

A. Robert Tyre (Bobby) Jones, Jr.

Q. What year did the Braves move to Atlanta?

A. 1966.

Q. Who produced more big league ball players than any other coach and is still known as "Father of Oglethorpe University Athletics"?

A. Frank B. Anderson, Sr.

Q. What Atlanta Falcon holds the highest pass completion percentage for one season?

A. Steve Bartkowski, 67.3 per cent (1984).

Q. The Gold Museum is located in which town?

A. Dahlonega.

Q. George M. Phillips, who officiated in Southern and Southeastern Conferences from 1929 to 1945, was known by what nickname?

A. "Pup."

———◆———

Q. Doug Sanders, winner of the five PGA Tournaments, is from what Georgia community?

A. Cedartown.

———◆———

Q. John W. Heisman coached at Georgia Tech during what time period?

A. 1904—1919.

———◆———

Q. Where in Columbus are the hulls of the ironclad *Jackson* and the gunboat *Chattahoochee* on display?

A. The Confederate Naval Museum.

———◆———

Q. John (Whack) Hyder, coach of Georgia Tech basketball for over two decades and professional baseball player for three years, is from what Georgia community?

A. Lula.

———◆———

Q. What Buena Vista-born ball player gained the distinction of being the greatest home run hitter in the Negro Baseball League?

A. Josh Gibson.

———◆———

Q. What city hosts the Ogeechee River Raft Race?

A. Statesboro.

Q. Atlanta athlete John Carson starred nine years as wide receiver for what NFL team?

A. Washington Redskins.

Q. What Athens native became the winningest active college tennis coach in America through 1979?

A. Dan Magill.

Q. Where was the birthplace of Rosey Grier, pro football player with the New York Giants?

A. Cuthbert.

Q. Georgia Tech coach Bill Fincher fashioned his own shoulder pads from what item?

A. A horse collar.

Q. Which millionaire's cottage now houses the Jekyll Island Museum?

A. The Rockefeller Cottage.

Q. Where is the Georgia Sports Hall of Fame located?

A. Atlanta.

Q. What Atlanta Hawk was a member of the gold-medal-winning United States Olympic Basketball Team in 1984?

A. Jon Koncak.

Q. What Macon native played for the Baltimore Colts from 1957 to 1967?

A. Jim Parker.

Q. What Columbus High athlete went on to captain the 1940 Bulldogs?

A. James Skipworth, Jr.

Q. What annual golfing event is held at Perry?

A. The Houston Lake Pro-Am Classic.

Q. Cordele is host to what July event?

A. Watermelon Festival.

Q. In what year was Georgia-born Ty Cobb elected to the National Baseball Hall of Fame?

A. 1936.

Q. What basketball player holds the all-time Atlanta Hawk high scoring record?

A. Bob Pettit, 20,880 points.

Q. What Commerce-born pitcher became the American League's Most Valuable Player in 1943?

A. Spurgeon (Spud) Chandler.

Q. Barnett native Jim Bagby, Sr. who won 31 games in 1920 to help lead Cleveland to its first American League pennant, was known by what nickname?

A. "Sarge".

———◆———

Q. What is the name of the authentic split sternwheel excursion riverboat based in Columbus?

A. *The Jubilee*.

———◆———

Q. Vince Dooley is the seven-time winner of what outstanding honor?

A. SEC Coach of the Year (1964, 66, 68, 76, 78, 80, 81).

———◆———

Q. What Atlanta Archer High student went on to Tennessee State and took the world of track by storm, winning the gold in the 1964 Olympics for the 200-meter dash?

A. Edith McGuire Duvall.

———◆———

Q. Georgia Tech is in what conference?

A. Atlantic Coast Conference.

———◆———

Q. Cochran is host to what May festival?

A. Gum Swamp Festival.

———◆———

Q. What Decatur High football coach won 42 games, losing only one conference game, from 1930 to 1933?

A. H. D. (Dickie) Butler.

Q. What coveted trophy was claimed by the Bulldogs in 1985 for being the SEC school with the most successful overall men's sports program?

A. Bernie Moore Trophy.

◆

Q. What city hosts the annual Crowe Springs Craftsmen's Fair in October?

A. Cartersville.

◆

Q. As a pioneer Georgia high school coach from 1912 to 1934, who organized the first basketball teams at Mineral Bluff, Omega, Pineview, Vienna and Norman Institute?

A. Joe H. Jenkins.

◆

Q. Where is the National Infantry Museum located, tracing the history of the infantry from the French and Indian War to the present?

A. Ft. Benning.

◆

Q. What Georgia Bulldog was known as "America's fastest man in water" in the 1950s, smashing records in the 1956 Melbourne Olympics?

A. Logan Reid Patterson.

◆

Q. What pro basketball player holds the all-time record for number of games played for the Hawks?

A. Bob Pettit, 792 games.

◆

Q. What two teams played the first game in the Atlanta-Fulton County Stadium on April 9, 1965?

A. The Milwaukee Braves defeated the Detroit Tigers, 6-3.

Q. Who were the two wealthiest owners of "millionaire cottages" on Jekyll Island?

A. John D. Rockefeller and J. P. Morgan.

———◆———

Q. What former Atlanta Brave stands second to Henry Aaron in most games played by a Brave in Atlanta?

A. Mike Lum.

———◆———

Q. In what 1981 bowl did the Bulldogs defeat Notre Dame?

A. Sugar Bowl.

———◆———

Q. Theo (Tiger) Flowers, known as "The Georgia Deacon," held what world championship title?

A. World middleweight boxing champion.

———◆———

Q. What city hosts the bi-annual Crackerland Country Fair?

A. Howard.

———◆———

Q. What Georgia coach is credited with introducing zone defense to the South?

A. H. J. Stegeman.

———◆———

Q. What educator, Baptist minister and coach played basketball, baseball and football and starred in track at Mercer University, and was known as "the greatest athlete in the South" from 1921 to 1925?

A. B. L. (Crook) Smith.

Q. Who served 17 years as the first Athletic Director of Atlanta schools, beginning in 1947, and was later to became the first Executive Director of the Atlanta-Fulton County Stadium?

A. Sidney Scarborough.

———◆———

Q. What type of horse race training facilities are located in Hawkinsville?

A. Harness Training Tracks.

———◆———

Q. Called "The Miracle Man," what Augusta native managed the Boston Braves from last place to a National League pennant and a World Series sweep?

A. George Tweedy Stallings.

———◆———

Q. For whom was Jekyll Island named?

A. Sir Joseph Jekyll, the largest contributor to Georgia's colonization.

———◆———

Q. What Gainesville High and Georgia athlete pitched for the 1959 Atlanta Crackers?

A. Jack Roberts.

———◆———

Q. Where can you participate in the July Appalachian Wagon Train?

A. Chatsworth.

———◆———

Q. Who was known for introducing numerous sportswriting innovations during his 1934—1976 career at the *Atlanta Constitution*?

A. Charles N. Roberts.

Q. In what year did John (Stumpy) Thomason, one of Atlanta Tech High's best halfbacks, lead Georgia Tech to a Rose Bowl championship?

A. 1928.

———◆———

Q. Who is said to be the most successful minor league operator of all time and was president and owner of the Atlanta Crackers from 1933 to 1959?

A. Earl Mann.

———◆———

Q. What is the name of the skiing resort located in Rabun County that offers natural and manmade snow?

A. Sky Valley.

———◆———

Q. Macon native Johnny Lee (Blue Moon) Odom pitched for what major league clubs during his 13-year playing career?

A. Kansas City A's, Oakland A's, Cleveland Indians, Chicago White Sox and Atlanta Braves.

———◆———

Q. Hank Aaron broke Babe Ruth's record for career home runs on what hit?

A. 715th.

———◆———

Q. What raceway is the home to the Canadian-American Challenge Cup?

A. Road Atlanta.

———◆———

Q. Known as major league's "Mr. Shortstop," what man who had his beginnings at Atlanta Tech High, played in four world series, five major league all-star games and managed the St. Louis Browns, Cardinals, and Chicago White Sox?

A. Martin (Marty) Marion.

Q. Where is the Monetary Museum located?

A. Atlanta.

Q. For what professional football team did William Thomas Stanfill play, after fine careers in Cairo and at the University of Georgia?

A. Miami Dolphins, 1969—1976.

Q. From Chamblee to Tokyo and Mexico City in the 1964 and 1968 Olympics, what Gold Medal track star became head track coach in 1975 at the West Point U.S. Military Academy?

A. Mel Pender.

Q. Cedartown-born Philips Brooks Douglas, who began his baseball career pitching for Rome and Macon, was best known by what nickname?

A. "Shufflin' Phil".

Q. Which Georgia Bulldog signed with the 1985 Falcons as a free agent?

A. Wayne Radloff.

Q. What city houses one of the largest indoor horse arenas in the southeast?

A. Unadilla.

Q. Where is the home court of the University of Georgia Bulldogs?

A. Georgia Coliseum.

Q. What Summerville native became "pro baseball's greatest fielding shortstop" in the 1930s?

A. Nolen Richardson.

———◆———

Q. What former Rome manager and major league ball player was known for having the smallest feet in the majors?

A. Myril Oliver Hoag.

———◆———

Q. What city is nicknamed "Golf Capital of the U.S."?
A. Augusta.

———◆———

Q. Where is the birthplace of John Milner, who played outfield and first base for 11 years with the New York Mets, Pittsburgh Pirates and Montreal Expos?

A. Atlanta.

———◆———

Q. What is the world-renowned resort located on Sea Island?

A. The Cloister.

———◆———

Q. In 1983 Leonidas S. Epps retired after a 34-year coaching career at what college?

A. Clark College, Atlanta.

———◆———

Q. What city is host to the annual Long County Wild Life Festival in October?

A. Ludoivici.

Q. What was Ty Cobb's lifetime batting average?

A. .367, the highest in baseball history.

———◆———

Q. What All-Star three-year halfback and two-year basketball standout went on to be inducted into the Georgia Tech Hall of Fame as halfback in 1947?

A. George Mathews.

———◆———

Q. What collection, one of the largest of its type in the world, is found at the Chickamauga National Military Park?

A. Fuller Gun Collection.

———◆———

Q. What Atlanta native served as Commissioner of the SEC Officials from 1947 through the 1970s?

A. George Gardner.

———◆———

Q. Who was the 1942 Decatur High "best all-around athlete" who later guided the Arkansas Razorbacks to top honors in football?

A. Frank Broyles.

———◆———

Q. What nautical ceremony is held each May in Darien?

A. The Blessing of the Fleet.

———◆———

Q. What Falcon holds the record for the most touchdowns by rushing in a single season?

A. Gerald Riggs, 1984.

Q. Golden Park is the home of which baseball team?

A. Columbus Astros.

◆

Q. What Villa Rica-born outfielder with the New York Yankees, Chicago White Sox, Detroit Tigers and the Brooklyn Dodgers was brother of batting star Harry Walker, son of Ewart Walker and nephew of Ernie Walker, all major leaguers?

A. Frederick E. (Dixie) Walker.

◆

Q. Which community hosts the Sunbelt Expo?

A. Moultrie.

◆

Q. What beverage was named for President Jimmy Carter's brother Billy?

A. Billy Beer.

◆

Q. What Atlanta Hawk holds the all-time field goal percentage record?

A. Mike Glenn, .553.

◆

Q. For 24 seasons, what man led the Bulldog golfers to be among the nation's best?

A. Howell Hollis.

◆

Q. What football player began at Georgia Tech in 1917 and became known as the second best Indian player in history?

A. Indian Joe (Joseph Napoleon Guyon), second only to Jim Thorpe.

Q. Who was the leading Lanier High athlete who played football center for Georgia and later coached at the university?

A. Quinton Lumpkin.

———◆———

Q. In what town were the first movie magazines of the Southeast displayed?

A. Montgomery.

———◆———

Q. What Falcon holds the record for most points scored in an individual season?

A. Mick Luckhurst, 114 points (1981).

———◆———

Q. What baseball Hall of Famer began his career in 1930 with the Southern Association, hitting .326 in 104 games with Atlanta?

A. Lucius Benjamen (Luke) Appling.

———◆———

Q. Which two weekends of the year is the Country Fair at Praters Mill, near Tunnel Hill held?

A. Mother's Day and Columbus Day weekends.

———◆———

Q. During his 11 seasons with Atlanta, what Falcon had won every football award and was very active in the Georgia Special Olympics and the founding of charity golf tournaments for the disadvantaged?

A. Tommy Nobis.

———◆———

Q. Demorest native John Mize played first base hitting .313 and slugging 2,000 hits for what three major league teams?

A. St. Louis Cards, New York Giants and New York Yankees.

Q. In 1905 the Detroit Tigers purchased Ty Cobb from Augusta of the South Atlantic League for what amount?

A. $500.

Q. Multi-millionaire J. P. Morgan had what type of sports facility built indoors on Jekyll Island?

A. Tennis court.

Q. Who is credited with hitting the longest home run at the Atlanta-Fulton County Stadium?

A. Willie Smith of the Chicago Cubs, 1969.

Q. What baseball player, discovered by Grantland Rice in Marietta, became Mayor of Roswell and one of the Dodgers best-known scouts?

A. George Napoleon Rucker.

Q. What Braves star won the 1982 and 1983 Most Valuable Player awards?

A. Dale Murphy.

Q. The nation's only manufacturer of golf ball molds is located in what community?

A. Perry.

Q. What are the two basic types of resort golf courses in Georgia?

A. Mountainous and seaside courses.

Q. What museum is located in the Keeper's Cottage of the St. Simons lighthouse?

A. Museum of Coastal History.

———◆———

Q. What Carrollton native had great success coaching track 42 years and produced two Olympic winners, Spec Towns and Bobby Packard?

A. Weems Baskin.

———◆———

Q. Who was the witty and popular sports columnist-analyst for the *Atlanta Journal*?

A. Harry Mehre.

———◆———

Q. Helen is noted for what annual aeronautical event?

A. Hot Air Balloon Festival.

———◆———

Q. What 19-year-old Georgia Bulldog, along with teammate Frankie Sinkwich, was a star on the team that won against UCLA 9-0 in the 1942 Rose Bowl?

A. Charley Trippi.

———◆———

Q. For how long did Young Stribling hold the world light-heavyweight title after a bout in Columbus on October 4, 1923?

A. Three hours, until the referee could escape a mob and reverse his decision.

———◆———

Q. Why did Ty Cobb refuse to room with Babe Ruth during an exhibition tour?

A. Because of rumors that Ruth had black heritage.

Q. Who was the youngest player to take part in a minor league game?

A. Joe Relford, a 12-year-old black batboy for the Fitzgerald Club in the Georgia State League on July 19, 1952.

Q. Gainesville High produced what sportsman who won the 1973 Master's Tournament and became the first Georgia golfer to earn over $100,000 on the pro tour in one season?

A. Tommy Aaron.

Q. What Atlanta Falcon holds the record for most yards gained in a single season?

A. William Andrews, 1,567 yards (1983).

Q. Where is the Military Museum located that features displays from the Civil War to present?

A. Hinesville.

Q. What was the nickname of 1925 Atlanta-born Harry Simpson, who played outfield for the Cleveland Indians, Kansas City Athletics and the New York Yankees?

A. "Suitcase."

Q. What Atlanta-born runner took the 1932 Olympics' Silver Medal in the 100 meters behind teammate Jesse Owens?

A. Ralph Metcalfe.

Q. What Atlanta-born athlete pitched one of the New York Giants' two victories in the 1951 World Series against the Yankees?

A. James Tolbert (Jim) Hearn.

Q. What is the name of the fieldhouse at Georgia College, Milledgeville?

A. Georgia Military Gym.

———◆———

Q. What Fitzgerald High School athlete was featured in Ripley's "Believe It or Not" after scoring ten touchdowns in one game?

A. Wright Bazemore.

———◆———

Q. What was the name of Ted Turner's yacht that earned him the 1977 America's Cup?

A. *Courageous.*

———◆———

Q. What coach became famous for producing such punters as Zeke Bratkowski, Johnny Rauch and Cliff Kimsey, as well as coaching Georgia kickers in the 1970s?

A. Bill Hartman, Jr.

———◆———

Q. Having played for Brooklyn, Cleveland and Pittsburgh from 1911 to 1927, what Mansfield-born pro baseball player was known for having the greatest pickoff move in baseball history?

A. Sherrod (Sherry) Smith.

———◆———

Q. What White County-born, Georgia Hall of Famer won the 1945 Kentucky Derby with the first race horse he ever owned?

A. Fred W. Hooper; horse, Hoop, Jr.

———◆———

Q. What city hosts the annual PGA Southern Open Golf Tournament?

A. Columbus.

Q. What quarterback led the Bulldogs to 1946 and 1948 SEC titles and went on to coach Oakland to the 1967 Super Bowl?

A. Johnny Rauch.

———◆———

Q. What sport was introduced by Scottish settlers at Darien in 1736?

A. Golf.

———◆———

Q. Where is the home court of the Atlanta Hawks?

A. The Omni.

———◆———

Q. What ball player started his career in Valdosta in 1947 and went on to play in the 1955 Brooklyn and 1960 Pittsburgh World Series?

A. Donald Albert (Tiger) Hoak.

———◆———

Q. What Bremen-born Yankee outfielder was known as "Babe Ruth's leg"?

A. Samuel Dewey Byrd.

———◆———

Q. Griffin school teacher Julia Elliott suggested the nickname for what Georgia team?

A. Falcons.

———◆———

Q. In what year did the AP and UPI choose Georgia as the National College Football Champions?

A. 1980.

Q. What tennis titleholder received the " Distinguished Citizen of Newton County" award for teaching tennis to Covington younsters?

A. Mary Louise Fowler.

———◆———

Q. What Thomaston-born ball player pitched only one complete major league game, a no-hitter?

A. Alva Lee (Bobo) Holloman, for the St. Louis Browns, 1953.

———◆———

Q. What is the seating capacity of Sanford Stadium?

A. 82,000, the fifth largest collegiate stadium.

———◆———

Q. What Decatur player was both a Los Angeles All-Pro linebacker and a Chicago Bear?

A. Larry Morris.

———◆———

Q. What Macon-born baseball manager is credited with developing stars Pete Rose, Tommy Helms, Lee May and Tony Perez?

A. David Bristol.

———◆———

Q. Which Georgia football team defeated the University of California at the 1929 Rose Bowl?

A. Georgia School of Technology Yellow Jackets.

———◆———

Q. Where is the birthplace of "Lil People" and Cabbage Patch Kids?

A. Babyland General Hospital, Cleveland.

Q. What former University of Georgia football player became the 1958 NFL's Rookie of the Year while playing for Pittsburgh?

A. Jimmy Orr.

———◆———

Q. Track coach Jimmy Carnes, President of Athletics Congress USA, is a native of what Georgia community?

A. Eatonton.

———◆———

Q. Who coached the Atlanta Falcons from 1974 to 1976?

A. Marion Campbell.

———◆———

Q. Fayette County's Cecil Travis was a member of what pro baseball team?

A. Washington Senators.

———◆———

Q. What Glynn County native won 30 national and international competitions for trap and skeet shooting?

A. Fred Misseldine.

———◆———

Q. Who holds the all-time personal fouls record for the Atlanta Hawks?

A. Bill Bridges, 2,575 fouls.

———◆———

Q. Athens High graduate Fran Tarkenton played for what two NFL teams?

A. Minnesota Vikings and New York Giants.

Q. What Atlanta businessman won nine matches to take the 1938 British Amateur tournament at Troon, Scotland?

A. Charlie Yates.

———◆———

Q. What Atlanta-born athlete was the only U.S. female to win a Gold Medal at the 1956 Melbourne Olympics?

A. Mildred McDaniel Singleton, world high jump record of 5'9¼".

———◆———

Q. What Tech Hall of Famer was the best offensive lineman for the Buffalo Bills from 1961 to 1969?

A. William L. (Billy) Shaw.

———◆———

Q. What two international yachting championships have been won by Ted Turner?

A. Scandinavian Gold Cup and the World Ocean Racing Championship in 1972.

———◆———

Q. What Marietta High School graduate became known as the Dean of American golf writers?

A. Oscar Bane (Pop) Keeler.

———◆———

Q. What all-around athlete was the first Georgia interior lineman to play pro for the Philadelphia Eagles in 1933?

A. L. Milton (Red) Leathers, Jr.

———◆———

Q. What Lincolnton-born ball player became a 1959 vice-president of the Washington Senators?

A. Joseph Walton Haynes.

Q. What Atlanta golfer received the International Championship Golf record by winning 15 consecutive holes?

A. Watts Gunn.

————◆————

Q. What winning Georgia college basketball coach retired in 1980?

A. James Boyd Scearce, Georgia Southern College, 501 victories, 284 defeats.

————◆————

Q. Nicholson native Claude Thomas Tolbert, who retired in 1940 after 20 winning coaching seasons at Atlanta Tech High, was known by what nickname?

A. Gabe.

————◆————

Q. What Atlanta-area coach developed championship teams and produced star athletes Marty Marion, Buster Mott and Franklin Brooks?

A. Henry L. (Hank) Langston.

————◆————

Q. Valdosta resident William L. Goodloe, Jr., a football player, recruiter and golfer was known by what nickname?

A. "Dynamite."

————◆————

Q. What Georgia Peach was known as the "Empress of Golf" during the 1920s?

A. Alexa Stirling Fraser.

————◆————

Q. Having attended school at Georgia, Vanderbilt and Young Harris, what man coached 52 years at Gainesville High and Georgia Tech and was known as "the man who never had an enemy"?

A. Joe Pittard.

SCIENCE & NATURE

C H A P T E R   S I X

Q. What manufacturing machine was invented in 1844 by Dr. John Gorrie of Columbus?

A. Ice machine.

———◆———

Q. What is the official state insect?

A. Honeybee.

———◆———

Q. Which community is nationally known for its sweet onions?

A. Vidalia.

———◆———

Q. What building material, principally made of oyster shells, is native to coastal Georgia?

A. Tabby.

———◆———

Q. Where is Patterson Planetarium located?

A. Columbus.

Q. What Old World species of large white bird may be seen in the pastures of coastal and southern Georgia?

A. Cattle Egret, *Bubulcus ibis*.

———◆———

Q. After continued plantings of cotton, acres of farmland are rendered useless due to the absence of what soil nutrient?

A. Nitrogen.

———◆———

Q. Where in Roswell is the wild animal rehabilitation program?

A. The Chattahoochee Nature Center.

———◆———

Q. What city is host to the Cotton Pickin' Antique Arts and Crafts Fair?

A. Gay.

———◆———

Q. What is the largest power company lake in the state?

A. Lake Oconee.

———◆———

Q. What is the estimated age of Lover's Oak in Brunswick?

A. Over 900 years.

———◆———

Q. What Turner County community was founded in 1877 and named for a large tree that came from the yard of Captain James Jackson Henderson?

A. Sycamore.

Q. Which newspaper was first printed on newsprint made from white slash pine?

A. *The Soperton News*, March 31, 1933.

———◆———

Q. What nut-producing tree was introduced to the state in 1905?

A. Paper-shell pecan.

———◆———

Q. What was Miss Lillian Carter's occupation?

A. Registered nurse.

———◆———

Q. What Terrell County town is known as the "World's Largest Spanish Peanut Market"?

A. Dawson.

———◆———

Q. What is the state flower?

A. Cherokee Rose.

———◆———

Q. The eastern part of White County is noted for what fire-resistant mineral?

A. Asbestos.

———◆———

Q. What is the deepest lake in the state?

A. Carter Lake, 400 feet.

Q. What is the state's largest fresh-water turtle, weighing up to 150 pounds?

A. Alligator snapper.

Q. What cotton industry process did Launcelot Johnston discover in 1830?

A. Making cotton seed oil.

Q. What is the name of the DeKalb County 20-acre natural wildlife refuge and petting zoo?

A. The Wild Life Trails at Stone Mountain.

Q. What is the local name for the wild hog of the swamp country?

A. Piney woods rooster.

Q. What was the chief building material used in the capitol building in Atlanta?

A. Indiana oolitic limestone.

Q. What is the official state fossil?

A. Shark tooth.

Q. Georgia produces approximately one-half of what national mineral?

A. Manganese ore.

Q. What geological feature, believed to be an ancient coastal sandbar, runs about 40 miles north and south along the eastern side of Okefenokee Swamp?

A. Trail Ridge.

———◆———

Q. What is the area of Okefenokee Swamp in square miles?

A. 681 square miles.

———◆———

Q. Why did President Franklin D. Roosevelt choose to retreat at Warm Springs, Georgia?

A. He believed the buoyant warm water would help his paralysis.

———◆———

Q. Where was the first school of forestry established?

A. University of Georgia, 1906.

———◆———

Q. Shell Bluff, on the Savannah River in Burke County, is noted for what type of fossils?

A. Oyster shells.

———◆———

Q. What four types of poisonous snakes are found in Georgia?

A. Rattlesnake, copperhead, water moccasin and coral snake.

———◆———

Q. What is the name of the Tifton living history village featuring agricultural displays of rural life before 1900?

A. Agrirama.

Q. Where are the headquarters of the American Camellia Society and its gardens located?

A. Marshallville.

Q. What wild orchid blooms in the Okefenokee Swamp?

A. Rose pogonias.

Q. What is the southern Georgia name given for the spreading or puffing adder because of its defense mechanism of playing dead?

A. Possum.

Q. What two nicknames, referring to food products, are given to the state?

A. The *Peach State* and the *Goober State*.

Q. What is Georgia's chief source of income?

A. Textile mills.

Q. Which is the highest earth-filled dam east of the Mississippi?

A. Carters Dam.

Q. In 1823 natural history researcher Samuel L. Mitchill began the scientific documentation of fossils by studying what creature found on Skidaway Island?

A. A giant ground sloth.

Q. The Crawford W. Long Medical Museum at Jefferson documents what medical discovery and advancement?

A. Anesthetics.

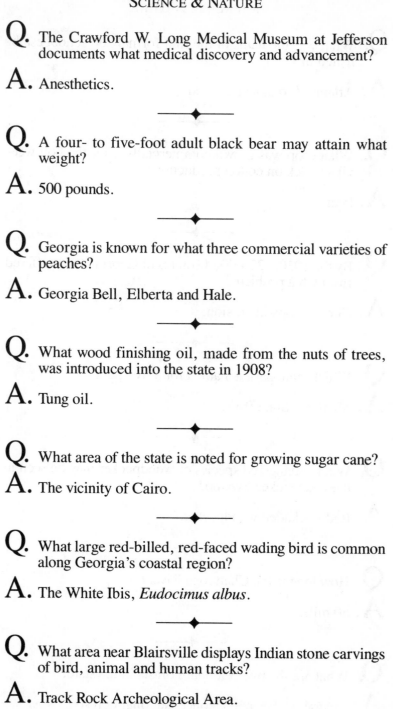

Q. A four- to five-foot adult black bear may attain what weight?

A. 500 pounds.

Q. Georgia is known for what three commercial varieties of peaches?

A. Georgia Bell, Elberta and Hale.

Q. What wood finishing oil, made from the nuts of trees, was introduced into the state in 1908?

A. Tung oil.

Q. What area of the state is noted for growing sugar cane?

A. The vicinity of Cairo.

Q. What large red-billed, red-faced wading bird is common along Georgia's coastal region?

A. The White Ibis, *Eudocimus albus*.

Q. What area near Blairsville displays Indian stone carvings of bird, animal and human tracks?

A. Track Rock Archeological Area.

Q. What was the name of the first formal zoo school established in 1960?

A. Atlanta Zoological Gardens.

———◆———

Q. What crop was grown commercially after the boll weevil's attack on cotton production?

A. Peanuts.

———◆———

Q. By the 1930s, 22,000,000 acres of Georgia land suffered from what problem?

A. Chronic topsoil erosion.

———◆———

Q. Which state park is named for a tree parasite?

A. Mistletoe State Park.

———◆———

Q. What endangered species of woodpecker may be seen in the Okefenokee Swamp?

A. Red-cockaded woodpecker.

———◆———

Q. How long is the Chattooga River?

A. 50 miles.

———◆———

Q. What are the two National Forests in the state?

A. Chattahoochee and Oconee National Forests.

Q. What museum is noted for its rare amethyst collection?

A. Weinman Mineral Center, near Cartersville.

———◆———

Q. Which Stephens County town is named for the Celtic word meaning "Island of Apples"?

A. Avalon.

———◆———

Q. What is the highest body of water in the state?

A. Conasauga Lake, Murray County, 3,200 feet above sea level.

———◆———

Q. How many miles of nature/hiking trails are located in the University of Georgia's Botanical Gardens?

A. Five.

———◆———

Q. What river did the Spanish name San Pedro?

A. Suwannee River.

———◆———

Q. Where was the first medical college chartered in 1828?

A. Augusta.

———◆———

Q. What did the Indians call the Okefenokee Swamp?

A. "Land of Trembling Earth."

Q. What is the name of the famous gorilla at the Atlanta Zoo?

A. Willie B.

———◆———

Q. What natural resource was harnessed to make Columbus a major manufacturing center?

A. Chattahoochee River.

———◆———

Q. What nocturnal marsupial is often served barbecued or baked with sweet potatoes?

A. Opossum.

———◆———

Q. What process caused peaches to become a major commercial crop after 1890?

A. Refrigeration.

———◆———

Q. What is the state tree?

A. Live oak.

———◆———

Q. In 1918, what Georgian originated the Flanders Field Memorial Poppy as the memorial flower of World War I?

A. Moina Bell Michael.

———◆———

Q. What plant forms the swamp country peat bogs?

A. Sphagnum moss.

Q. Where can the original Apollo 6 Space Capsule be seen?

A. Fernbank Science Center, Atlanta.

———◆———

Q. Who is credited with developing the process of making newsprint from pine?

A. Dr. Charles Herty, 1932.

———◆———

Q. What is the state bird?

A. Brown Thrasher.

———◆———

Q. What city hosts the Fall Leaf Festival?

A. Cleveland.

———◆———

Q. In the 1930s the area around Griffin became prominent for producing what crop?

A. Pimientos.

———◆———

Q. What is the name of the wildlife preserve in Albany that provides elevated walkways for the viewing of animals in their natural habitat?

A. Chehaw Wild Animal Park.

———◆———

Q. What is the largest natural spring in the state?

A. Radium Springs in Dougherty County.

Q. What is another name for the Little Grand Canyon, west of Lumpkin, in Stewart County?

A. Providence Canyon.

◆

Q. In what year was the "Big Fire" in the Okefenokee Swamp?

A. 1844.

◆

Q. What Atlanta pharmacist invented Coca-Cola?

A. John Pemberton.

◆

Q. How many acres of stacked lumber is maintained on inventory at the Del-Cook Lumber Company of Cook County, the largest lumber company in the eastern United States?

A. 80.

◆

Q. What unusual geological formation is located in the area of Albany?

A. Fossil sand dunes.

◆

Q. What city houses one of the twenty-five national test gardens for All American Roses?

A. Thomasville.

◆

Q. What is the largest reptile found in the state?

A. Alligator.

Q. What Macon County man originated the Elberta peach?

A. Samuel B. Rumph.

———◆———

Q. The horses that pulled the first streetcars of Atlanta were soon replaced by what other animals?

A. Red-tailed Mexican mules.

———◆———

Q. What flower is believed to grow only within a 50-mile radius of Stone Mountain?

A. Confederate Yellow Daisy.

———◆———

Q. What is the largest national wildlife refuge in the eastern United States?

A. Okefenokee National Wildlife Refuge.

———◆———

Q. What two rivers originate in the Okefenokee Swamp?

A. St. Marys and Suwannee.

———◆———

Q. What mineral is refined from Georgia's production of bauxite?

A. Aluminum.

———◆———

Q. In 1842, what method for painless surgery was introduced in Jefferson by Dr. Crawford W. Long?

A. The use of ether as an anesthetic.

Q. What lake is formed by the Chattahoochee and Flint Rivers at the Jim Woodruff Dam?

A. Lake Seminole.

———◆———

Q. What variety of cotton was introduced from the Bahama Islands in 1786?

A. Sea-island cotton.

———◆———

Q. What is the name of the 146-acre retail and wholesale outlet for Georgia farmers?

A. Atlanta State Farmers Market.

———◆———

Q. What river was made famous by Stephen Foster's *Old Folks At Home*?

A. Suwannee.

———◆———

Q. What memorial in Washington, D.C. is built of Georgian marble?

A. The Lincoln Memorial.

———◆———

Q. In what year was the Okefenokee Swamp declared a wildlife refuge?

A. 1937.

———◆———

Q. What agricultural region is centered in Ashburn?

A. The peanut belt.

Q. Where are marine exhibits and a "petting" aquarium located?

A. Coastal exhibit room, Georgia Department of Natural Resources, Brunswick.

———◆———

Q. How many state parks are located in Georgia?

A. 43.

———◆———

Q. What is the acreage of Stone Mountain?

A. 583.

———◆———

Q. What common trait is shared by the sundew, yellow butterwort, pitcher and bladderwort plants of the moist, swampy areas?

A. They are insect eaters.

———◆———

Q. What mineral was mined in colonial days from deposits near Augusta and Macon for use at the Wedgewood Pottery in England?

A. Kaolin, a high grade clay.

———◆———

Q. What small, armored mammal was introduced from the Southwest and Mexico in the early 1960s?

A. Armadillo.

———◆———

Q. What is the state's highest recorded temperature?

A. 112 degrees F (44 degrees C), Louisville, July 24, 1952.

Q. Which Corp-of-Engineer-built lake holds the national record for annual visits?

A. Lake Lanier.

———◆———

Q. What is the popular name for the official state mineral, staurolite?

A. "Fairy Crosses" or "Fairy Stones."

———◆———

Q. What was the first large cash crop to be planted in the sea islands?

A. Indigo.

———◆———

Q. What is Georgia's official state fish?

A. Largemouth Bass.

———◆———

Q. Country music performer Roy Drusky holds a degree in what field?

A. Veterinary medicine.

———◆———

Q. In 1974, the Chattooga River was placed under what federal protection plan?

A. The Wild and Scenic Rivers Act.

———◆———

Q. Stone Mountain granite was used for what Caribbean university building?

A. The University of Havana.

Q. What member of the hare family is noted for its swimming ability in the swamp country?

A. Marsh Rabbit.

———◆———

Q. What city hosts the Putnam County Dairy Festival?

A. Eatonton.

———◆———

Q. In what Savannah area may indigenous animals be seen in their natural habitat?

A. Oatland Island.

———◆———

Q. What grayish stemmed, rootless plant can be seen hanging from trees and power lines across the southern portion of the state?

A. Spanish Moss, *Tillandsia usneoides*.

———◆———

Q. What does the Greek word *georgia* mean?

A. Agriculture.

———◆———

Q. Where can one of the largest reptile collections in America be viewed?

A. Atlanta Zoo, Grant Park.

———◆———

Q. What Lincoln County mathematician and engineer predicted the total eclipse of the sun on May 28, 1900, fifty years before it happened?

A. Thomas P. Ashmore (1812—1884).

Q. What Texas bird may be found in some concentration in southeastern coastal Georgia?

A. Plain Chachalaca, *Ortalis vetula*.

◆

Q. Under what circumstance was ether first used as an anesthetic?

A. Dr. Crawford W. Long administered it to remove a cyst from the neck of James Venable.

◆

Q. The interconnecting tidal rivers and creeks of the inland portion of Jekyll and St. Simons Islands are known by what name?

A. Marshes of Glynn.

◆

Q. What is the state's most valuable farm product?

A. Broilers.

◆

Q. By 1763, what river was the western boundary of Georgia?

A. Mississippi River.

◆

Q. Which state park is known as the "Grand Canyon of North Georgia"?

A. Cloudland Canyon State Park.

◆

Q. What city hosts the Georgia Marble Festival?

A. Jasper.

Q. What 1848 communications hook-up installed from Augusta to Columbus linked Washington, D.C. with New Orleans?

A. The state's first telegraph.

———◆———

Q. What is Georgia's official state wildflower?

A. Azalea.

———◆———

Q. What is the daily water output of Blue Springs, at the foot of Pine Mountain in Harris County?

A. One million gallons.

———◆———

Q. What county housed the first tannery?

A. Lincoln County.

———◆———

Q. What city produces more granite monuments than any other city in the world?

A. Elberton.

———◆———

Q. What gave Blue Bluff in Burke County its name?

A. Blue-gray glauconitic clay.

———◆———

Q. Which city is known as the "Camellia City of the South"?

A. Thomson.

Q. What Georgia site provided the granite that was used in part of the Panama Canal construction?

A. Stone Mountain.

———◆———

Q. What scenic creek in the Chattahoochee National Forest drops 600 feet in less than one mile?

A. Frogtown Creek.

———◆———

Q. What is the official state gem, named in 1976?
A. Quartz.

———◆———

Q. What is the official state game bird, named in 1970?
A. Bobwhite Quail.

———◆———

Q. Georgia ranks second in the national production of what building stone?

A. Marble.

———◆———

Q. What price did large alligator skins bring in 1906?
A. $1.50.

———◆———

Q. Where may special trails for heart patients and the visually impaired be found?

A. Fernbank Science Center, Atlanta.

Q. Where is the University of Georgia Marine Institute located?

A. Sapelo Island.

---◆---

Q. What is the acreage of the bald on Brasstown Bald?

A. 3/4 of an acre.

---◆---

Q. What nutrient-rich plant, producing up to ten tons to the acre, is important to the ecological food chain of the coastal region?

A. Marsh grass.

---◆---

Q. What flowering shrub is known for its strychnine-like poison?

A. Yellow Jasmine.

---◆---

Q. What insect first attacked the cottonfields in 1921?

A. Boll Weevil.

---◆---

Q. Georgia is the national leader in the production of what porous claylike material used in various industrial processes?

A. Fuller's earth.

---◆---

Q. What large plant-eating marine mammal found in the coastal waters may have given rise to mermaid legends?

A. Manatee or Sea Cow.

---◆---

Q. Forests cover approximately what percentage of Georgia?

A. 70 per cent.

Q. What is Georgia's most valuable cash crop?

A. Peanuts.

Q. What is the local name for the dense swamp area in upper Laurens County?

A. Cow Hell.

Q. What internationally-known naturalist and wildlife expert designed the Black Rhinoceros exhibit at the Atlanta Zoo?

A. Jim Fowler.

Q. Who was Georgia's first woman doctor?

A. Dr. Loree Florence of Lincoln County.

Q. A giant 300-foot diameter mound on Sapelo Island, typifying Georgia's first Indian mounds, is composed of what material?

A. Saltwater shells.

Q. The Museum of Arts and Sciences and the Mark Smith Planetarium are located in which city?

A. Macon.

Q. What was the original name of the machine known as the cotton gin?

A. Cotton engine.

Q. The grounds of Callanwolde Fine Arts Center in Atlanta, the former home of Charles Howard Candler, past-president of Coca-Cola, were designed by what famous landscape artist?

A. Frederick Law Olmstead, designer of New York City's Central Park.

◆

Q. What is the function of the cotton gin?

A. It removes cotton fibers from the cotton seed.

◆

Q. What famous battleship was constructed from the live oaks on Gascoigne Bluff?

A. "Old Ironsides," U.S. Frigate *Constitution*.

◆

Q. What river separates Little St. Simons Island from St. Simons Island?

A. Hampton River.

◆

Q. What museum, opened in 1981, displays exhibits, artifacts and educational information one of northeast Georgia's largest industries?

A. Elberton Granite Museum and Exhibit.

◆

Q. Who was the first physician of Stewart County?

A. Dr. Bryan Bedingfield.

◆

Q. What type of federal project, featuring 26 large tank aquariums, is located near Millen?

A. National Fish Hatchery.

Q. What tree, common in the southern swamps and noted for its "knees," may reach a height of 120 feet?

A. Cypress.

———◆———

Q. The first bauxite discovery in the United States in 1887 was made near which northwestern community?

A. Rome.

———◆———

Q. What Georgia city calls itself the "quail hunting capital of the world"?

A. Albany.

———◆———

Q. What ethnic group was extensively researched in the 1890s by James Mooney for the Smithsonian Institute's Bureau of American Ethnology?

A. Cherokee Indians.

———◆———

Q. What is the acreage of the Okefenokee Swamp?

A. 438,000 acres.

———◆———

Q. What lizard is the swiftest and most elusive in the state?

A. The six-lined race runner or race nag.

———◆———

Q. What is Georgia's national rank in pecan production?

A. First.

Q. What is the second-ranking cash crop in Georgia?

A. Soybeans.

———◆———

Q. Where is the state's largest apple-growing center?

A. Cornelia.

———◆———

Q. What is the common name for the large marshes in Okefenokee Swamp?

A. Prairies.

———◆———

Q. What is the geological feature created by the division between the Piedmont Plateau and the Coastal Plain?

A. The Fall Line.

———◆———

Q. Georgia is the second national producer of what soft, heavy, silver-colored metallic element?

A. Barite, from which barium is processed.

———◆———

Q. What type of trees were planted by colonists to help establish a silk industry in Georgia?

A. Mulberry.

———◆———

Q. What national park is the oldest, largest and most visited?

A. Chickamauga National Military Park.

Q. What is the real name of the Georgia "Goat Man," who drove a cart pulled by goats between Macon and Monteagle, Tennessee in the 1940s, 50s and 60s?

A. Chesney McCartney.

———◆———

Q. What brightly colored, red, blue and yellow-green bird may be seen along the coastal regions in the summer?

A. Painted Bunting, *Passerina ciris*.

———◆———

Q. What type of flower, in over 400 varieties, is shipped throughout the world from Perry?

A. Day Lilies.

———◆———

Q. Where was Georgia's first paper mill located?

A. Scull Shoals.

———◆———

Q. What name does tradition say was given to the Suwannee River by the Maya Indians from the Yucatan?

A. Water Beloved of the Sun God.

———◆———

Q. What annual Atlanta event benefits the Henrietta Egleston Hospital for critically ill children?

A. The Festival of Trees, December.

———◆———

Q. Who was the Quaker naturalist and trail blazer in northeastern Georgia over 200 years ago?

A. William Bartram.

Q. Cumberland Island has been given what distinction?

A. National Seashore, 1972.

———◆———

Q. Which historic site was once owned by Tiffany's of New York?

A. Graves Mountain, southwest of Lincolnton.

———◆———

Q. Where is a 38-foot model of a Loblolly Pine located?

A. Southern Forest World, Waycross.

———◆———

Q. What is the annual apple harvest in Gilmer County?

A. 200,000 bushels.

———◆———

Q. What Dalton company had its former offices in the Crown Gardens and Archives?

A. Crown Cotton Mills.

———◆———

Q. What rare species of small tree was discovered growing naturally only in Georgia by John and William Bartram in 1765?

A. Lost Camelia, *Franklinia* or *Gordonia Altamaha*.

———◆———

Q. What is the actual name of the color-changing lizard known as the American chameleon?

A. The green anole.

Q. What is the name of the world's smallest fish that is found in the Okefenokee Swamp?

A. Pygmy killifish.

Q. What is the collective name of the 153-foot waterfall on Curtis Creek and the 50-foot waterfall on York Creek?

A. Anna Ruby Falls.

Q. Which state park is located in Cobb and Fulton counties?

A. Chattahoochee Palisades State Park.

Q. What was the production level of corn in the state at the outbreak of the Civil War in 1860?

A. 30 million bushels.

Q. What is the name of the Indian archeological site near Macon?

A. Old Ocmulgee Fields.

Q. Trees of foreign origin, including the tung and Chinese pistachio, surround the courthouse of which city?

A. Brunswick.

Q. What Savannah museum features a walk-through human heart replica?

A. The Science Museum.

Q. The southern Indians enjoyed the black fruit of what common American palm?

A. Saw palmetto.

Q. What is the name of the world's most advanced greenhouse complex featured at Callaway Gardens?

A. John A. Sibley Horticultural Center.

Q. What is the Creek Indian translation of Lochochee Creek in Terrell County?

A. "Little Turtle."

Q. McCranier's Turpentine Still is located near which community?

A. Willacoochee.

Q. What Georgian legless lizard is often mistaken for a snake?

A. Glass lizard.

Q. How many ingredients are found in Coca-Cola?

A. 15.

Q. What is the lowest recorded temperature on Brasstown Bald?

A. -27 degrees F.